An Engineer of Coincidence

A Memoir

An Engineer of Coincidence

A Memoir

Edward S. Fort OBE

Nine Elms Books

First published in 2017 by Nine Elms Books Ltd
Unit 6B
Clapham North Arts Centre
26-32 Voltaire Road
London SW4 6DH

Email: inquiries@bene-factum.co.uk
ISBN: 978-1-910533-23-9

Cover portrait photograph by Jonty Wilde :: www.jontywilde.com
Portrait page ii by Nathan D'Amour :: www.nathandamour.co
Photographs cover and pages 115, 116, 160 by Sally Armstrong :: www.solentpics.com
Photographs cover and page 146 by Max Bretherton
Photograph cover, hot air balloon, by Steve Wass

Design, photography and typesetting by John Hartley Associates Ltd, BB8 7EF UK
studio@johnhartley.co.uk

Printed in the UK by Henry Ling Ltd, Dorchester, Dorset

Dedication

I have to dedicate this work to the memory of my family, and to the Forts of earlier ages who were the foundation and building blocks of our traditions and principles. The ones who touched me most were my parents, of course. Ever supportive, encouraging and passing on the family standards. They got me started in life, in education, in career and in business. Brother Robert, too, was always there working with me helping the company to grow with his intelligence and skill. I am sure they would all be proud of everything that has been achieved that now carries the family name.

CONTENTS

16. A VERY SPECIAL LADY

17. A VERY MEMORABLE LADY

18. HEALTH IS WEALTH

19. THE DUTY OF WEALTH

20. CONCERNS FOR THE FUTURE

Foreword
by
Lord Lee of Trafford DL FCA

"An Engineer of Coincidence" – Ted Fort's memoir – is far more than "a rags-to-riches" story. It is the life history of a very human being laid bare, sometimes in frank and excruciating detail, of pride and pleasures, of love and loneliness. At times his self-deprecation can be brutal "I am sometimes regarded as a bit of a joke – 'Here comes Old Clogs again, the metal-basher from the Midlands' – they can't even get that right" – on his progress from Lancashire mill town to Beaulieu, and his recounting the Duke of Edinburgh saying, "Fort – you're swanking" and walking off, after Ted tells him that he has shaken the Queen's hand many times! There are two words which for me are the key to this very successful life – "detail" and "determination". The precise recording of his trading activities when as a youngster he owned 70 hens – selling eggs to the Milk Marketing Board, and the very detailed drawings of Fort Vale's first valves, and the determination and ambition to successfully win so many awards both for exports and also in the very competitive world of sailing. One could be forgiven for thinking that pride in making the Sunday Times Rich List, luxury homes in the south of France and other trappings of prosperity suggest a rather selfish and self-centred individual, but this would be manifestly unfair and would ignore Ted's deep commitment to the training and employment of apprentices, the medical facilities for employees at Fort Vale, and the creation of his two charitable foundations – The Fort Foundation and The Beaulieu Beaufort Foundation – endeavouring to mirror what his admired textile giants of earlier times did for their communities in terms of workers' houses, hospitals and water supplies. The final chapter "Concerns for the Future" reflects his worries for our planet and our environment – the responsibility we all have to future generations.

It is has been a great privilege to have known Ted as I have over many years and to have benefitted from his generosity and friendship. I can only endorse what Susan, his great love and companion over twenty-five years, wrote in a personal letter to him as she faced a serious medical procedure – "I am very proud of you. A truly special man. A good man. Kind, honest, caring and loving. An honest and generous human being who has been a great achiever and yet retains his values and generosity to others". All who know him will appreciate and echo these sentiments. With Engineering at the very core of Ted's life I think this memoir could be fairly described as a "riveting" read!

Lord Lee of Trafford DL FCA
September 2016

Introduction

It must be natural, I suppose, to reminisce more as one gets older. At least, I hope it is and not a sign of approaching senility!

Standing in front of my house in the New Forest, gazing down the long, sloping lawn; watching the morning light bringing the shimmering surface of the Beaulieu River to life; I wonder how on earth we got here – how did it happen?

It is not now uncommon for me to have such a moment. It can happen in the grounds of the house; wandering around the woodlands; admiring the trees we have planted over the years or listening to a woodpecker high in the foliage.

It can happen at the factory in Lancashire – at Fort Vale Engineering – standing on the gallery overlooking the machine shop. I look at the regimented rows of the state-of-the-art machines - tended by the skilled operators, programmed by computer and fed by robots – and wonder some more. How on earth did we get to here? I can, I admit, get a little emotional in these moments.

And then the analysis starts to take hold – as it would with any engineer. This immaculate, cutting-edge manufacturing facility with its high standards in quality, precision, safety, performance and presentation stems from me – from the early days and the standards laid down in the very beginning. It's a most moving realisation.

How did it happen? How did a Lancashire lad who used to wear clogs and clatter on the cobbled streets of a mill town get to this? A boy in a family that lived on a farm with an outside loo and no electricity? A lad near the bottom of the class at school who kept hens and sold eggs for spending money?

It was, of course, the fact that I gained an engineering apprenticeship at Rolls Royce. That defined exactly the path to be followed. As soon as I started there I knew, as precisely as we machine metal now, that I was going to be an engineer.

What followed was a remarkable series of events determined by fate and by coincidences. The skill, I believe, is in what we make of coincidences. They always have consequences but when the consequence is turned into a positive pivotal moment in one's life it can have a monumental effect.

Standing on my jetty, looking over the river at the boats moored on the trots, I am reminded of one such monumental, pivotal moment. A white-painted sloop of traditional lines is moored about four buoys down from the jetty. Her name is Sinbad of Cowes. I knew her as Sinbad of Abersoch it was she who halted – no, postponed – my engineering career. It was on board Sinbad that I learnt from experienced, older men more about real life – the nitty-gritty. On returning to the north of England, after a voyage of many months, it was my working for the company owned by one of the sailors, the owner of Sinbad, that prompted the formation of my own company. Ultimately, that company created the resources for me to be able to live here, by the river.

The yacht was sold many, many years ago but, some sixty years later, there she is, Sinbad, moored at the bottom of my garden, in the south of England, many miles from Abersoch. Now that is a coincidence.

A little wealth does allow for some luxury and higher living standards, it's true, but it does come with a responsibility, to my mind. I like to think we are able to give deserving others a helping hand to achieve a pivotal moment in their own lives. My two charitable foundations – the Fort Foundation and the Beaulieu Beaufort Foundation – have been set up to give that little extra help to allow the individual to progress where they might not otherwise succeed.

My own key pivotal moment – the spark – was my apprenticeship at Rolls Royce. It was of such importance that it is hard to over-emphasise. I have always promoted apprenticeship schemes to help the young progress and have always had one in place at Fort Vale. It gives me immense satisfaction to see past apprentices continuing to work at the company for many years – some for nearly fifty years – some reaching director level.

It was an apprenticeship which got me started on a successful business career – needing lots of hard work, yes, and a great team – but I have loved doing it and living life to the full on the way (and still do!).

And if a Lancashire lad in clogs can do it.......?

Good luck.

Ted Fort
September 2016

Acknowledgements

I am most grateful to all those who have had the patience and goodwill in helping me to put together this tome. I could never have done this alone.

Help with my memory has come from family members, colleagues from work, sailing companions and good friends. They have also contributed many of the photographs from their own collections or those taken especially for me – and here I must mention Sally Armstrong in particular for some of the super sailing images and those of dear Susan at home – they were close friends.

My sincere thanks go to all involved.

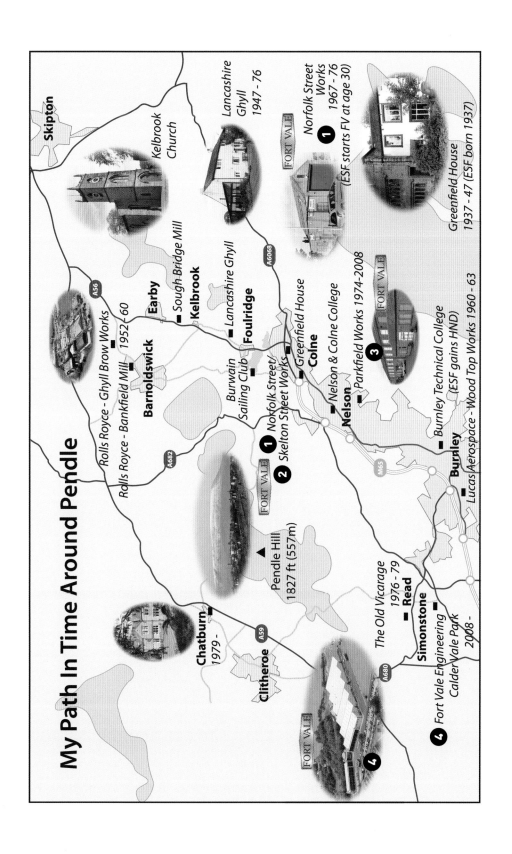

My Path In Time Around Pendle

Skipton

Kelbrook Church

Lancashire Ghyll
1947 - 76

FORT VALE

Norfolk Street
Works
1 1967 - 76
(ESF starts FV at age 30)

Greenfield House
1937 - 47 (ESF born 1937)

A56

Rolls Royce - Ghyll Brow Works 1952 - 60

Rolls Royce - Bankfield Mill

Earby

South Bridge Mill

Kelbrook

Barnoldswick

Lancashire Ghyll

Foulridge

A6068

Burwain
Sailing Club

Greenfield House

Colne

Norfolk Street/
Skelton Street Works

Nelson & Colne College

Parkfield Works 1974-2008

FORT VALE

A682

1
Norfolk Street/
Skelton Street Works

FORT VALE

2
Skelton Street Works

Nelson

3

Burnley Technical College
(ESF gains HND)

M65

Burnley

Lucas Aerospace - Wood Top Works 1960 - 63

Pendle Hill
1827 ft (557m)

The Old Vicarage
1976 - 79

Read

Simonstone

A680

Fort Vale Engineering
Calder Vale Park
2008 -

FORT VALE

4

Chatburn
1979 -

A59

Clitheroe

My story revolves around the witch country of Pendle Hill. From my family roots in Kelbrook, through Colne, Nelson, Burnley, Chatburn and the final location for Fort Vale Engineering in Simonstone, so close to my earlier house in Read.

Chapter 1

The Early Formative Years

Until I reached the age of ten, our family had a most exclusive address – Greenfield House, Greenfield Road, Colne. The truth of the matter is that we simply rented a 19th century cottage attached to the original, 16th century Greenfield House and in no way did we live in the big house itself, which is the surviving cross-wing of a formerly larger house. It has seven-light, stone mullion windows reflecting the high status of the original occupants and was made a Grade II listed building in 1953.

The rent was 15 shillings a week, or around £43 in today's value. (For those not around in the pre-metric currency days, one pound consisted of 240 pence in 'old money': there were 12 pence in a shilling and 20 shillings in a pound, therefore. Pounds shillings and pence were written as £1.1s.1d.)

There was no central heating in our cottage in the 1930's of course and the windows were single glazed. Thick, icy layers of frost formed on the inside of the glass panes on cold nights. A very early memory, probably my earliest, is of tossing and turning in my cot, freezing, in the cold bedroom. I'd tossed away the bedclothes somehow and could not sort them out nor raise my parents with my crying. I must have

Left: An early photograph showing Greenfield Cottage to the right of Greenfield House.

Above: Father looking very pleased on the arrival of young Ted

Below: Everyone had to carry a gas mask going to school

been very young indeed but the memory is still with me, all these years later, of how cold I was that night.

The cottage, though, was fine with a pleasant garden and a small river running behind. It allowed for plenty of fun for young lads. We had an open coal fire and a bath – a real bath, not a tin tub in front of the fire as in a lot of the local houses in the area. There were two bedrooms so that younger brother, Robert, and I slept in the back and Mother and Father in the front.

Historically, Greenfield is a township of Colne in the north east corner of Lancashire, an area famous for the textile industry and particularly cotton weaving. The consequences of the demise of this local industry have been a big factor in my life, popping up incessantly in one way or another, as you will discover.

Father trained as a 'tackler' looking after the engineering side of a mill's operation, the looms themselves and the driving mechanisms. A tackler was an engineer in practice and was paid a bit more than a weaver. Eventually Father had a partnership in a commissioning mill in Clarence Street and became secretary of the local textile society. It must have been a position of note, I think, and I used to feel very proud as a young boy when sent out with a large bundle of letters to post for Father. It also made me feel important too.

There was a routine to life in Greenfield Road – as there must have been in any street neighbourhood in a Lancashire town in those days. The milk was delivered each morning by horse and cart. Little old ladies would hurry up the street to wait for the milkman, knowing exactly where he would draw up next with his cart. They would gather at their regular point each morning and discuss the latest news until he arrived. I remember pouring what we called a 'gill' of milk (pronounced 'Jill') – which was a quarter of a pint. (However, and I don't know why, if you asked for a gill in a local pub, you were served with a half pint of beer, not a quarter.)

My first school was at the top of the steep, cobbled street leading from our house up to Primet Junior School as it then was. We wore steel-soled clogs that clattered on the cobbles. These had rigid wooden soles and leather uppers. The metal 'irons' on the soles, rather like horse shoes, would create sparks when kicked down hard on the grit stone cobbles or sandstone footpath flags (as the vernacular for paving stones has it). If the footpath was steep enough, they would also act like runners on a sledge and allow one to skate down the flags. Shoes were saved for the weekend and, especially, for Sundays. My father actually had a cobbler's last on which to repair and re-sole our clogs.

These early years overlapped with World War Two. I hated the thin string of my gas mask which could cut into my neck on the way up that hill on the walk to school. Everyone had to carry a gas mask during the

Left: My first school, now called Primet Primary School

war years. Sometimes, in the evenings, we would hear distant bombs landing on the Manchester area and we would be taken down to the cellar as a precaution.

Food was rationed and the memory of eating in those days conjures up images of beetroot and potatoes! We did, however, have some farming relations at Spring House Farm outside Pateley Bridge, near Harrogate. We used to go there at haymaking time for a 'holiday' to help on the farm. There was no tractor on the farm and the work in the fields was all with horse-drawn machinery or by hand. Tractors only began to appear on local farms following the war. We had to rake all the rows of grass into lines in the many fields and then turn them, periodically, to help the grass dry. The grass was then collected into tall, conical stacks called 'pikes' before being loaded onto a trailer and taken to the barn. Making pikes was the Yorkshire method whereas in Lancashire the hay or grass was thrown directly onto the carts.

Although there wasn't food rationing on the farm, we always started the meal with large portions of Yorkshire pudding to fill us up. Meat and eggs were available there and were a real treat for us after life in Colne. We could always go out and shoot rabbits and pigeons, too, if we needed extra meat.

The nearby, high moorland would sometimes catch out a bomber returning to base from a mission over France or Germany – usually a British aircraft but sometimes a German one would come down, creating a rush of locals out to capture the crew. A walk up onto Greenhow Hill with Father to find the wreckage of a crashed plane would be quite exciting for us as young boys even though it was a long way to the crash sites. We were mesmerised by the size of the engines and the intricate, metal airframes. They were so unusual as nothing

Below: I revisit the hill leading from home up to my first school

remotely similar existed in our day-to-day life. Robert and I would walk on the wings without appreciating the human cost and suffering associated with the destruction.

Although nearly forty miles from Colne, Father would often cycle to Spring House to collect black market food to keep us going. This was all pretty risky during the war, as he would have been landed with a serious fine if stopped by the police and found to be carrying black market rations. He was very industrious and had made bicycles for all of us. We all did a lot of cycling then. Mother, too, was extremely dexterous and had made a special saddlebag for his bicycle to carry the rations from Pateley Bridge.

These were days when most goods were much too expensive for ordinary folk or not available at all. It was a time of 'make do and mend' in the true sense. We were fortunate in having the mill on Clarence Street – and in having capable parents who knuckled down when required. We made our own tablecloths, sheets, handkerchiefs, etc. at the mill and Father repaired the soles of our shoes from worn out leather power take-off belts that drove the looms.

Mother also painted pottery, made leatherwork items for sale and produced many other handcrafted knick-knacks for a little more income. She also made a tent that I used on our holidays. We did have holidays – sometimes in Blackpool, Southport or Llandudno – but in those days we would take our own food to the boarding house due to rationing still being in force.

Running a mill also meant that Father was in a reserved occupation so didn't join the Forces. Instead, he became a local air raid warden. All the Fort family members were in reserved occupations – either through textiles or farming – and none were called up.

One of my greatest friends, in those days and still, is David Huggins. He lived in a large house just over the road from Christiana Hartley Maternity Hospital where I was born. His father was the vicar at Christ Church at the top of Phillips Lane, next to Primet Primary School. Our house was on the route from the Huggins' house to the church. As the vicar came past, clutching David by the hand, he would grab me with the other hand and walk us both up the hill to church. We would be around four or five years old when this ritual began, which occurred each Sunday. Very often it would be three times a day – morning service; Sunday school in the afternoon and evening service.

On one occasion I had to pump the organ bellows, which was a tiring task for a ten year old. I only did it once, which was, I believe, because I kept hitting the stops when pumping away with the wooden handle, creating loud banging and clattering noises throughout each hymn.

Strangely, and I never discovered quite why, my parents never did come to church with us on a Sunday and I only ever remember being with them in church for christenings, weddings or funerals – never at any other time. I don't think it was that they weren't religious – just not worshippers.

I myself was never very religious, as such, but I do recognise the value in the moral standards that the church established. And, as my Uncle Phillip said, "Without the church, all we have is the State."

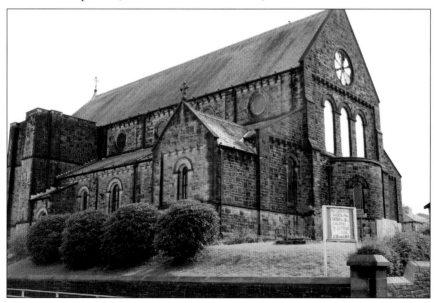

Left: Christ Church, where David Huggin's father was the vicar

I have always supported the church. Phillip Oldfield, Uncle Phillip, was Mother's sister Doris' husband and gave me a lot of useful advice.

David Huggins and I would get up to the usual boyish activities – such as building a dam in the river behind the cottage and getting thoroughly wet and muddy, much to our mothers' distress. We once staked out brother Robert with ropes and pegs.

As the modern age was still not upon us, there were no televisions or computers, of course. We did have electricity but no telephone or motorcar. Entertainment was homemade. David would turn up at the back steps and ask Mother if I could play out. Sometimes the answer might be "No, Edward has jobs to do." Usually, though, he was treated to a home-made biscuit. David recalls Mother as "... always very friendly and cheerful although the war time years must have been very hard for parents with everything in short supply and books of coupons for rationed food and clothing".

We did not really have a grasp of what the war was all about at that age but did pick up on certain elements – such as the Japanese water torture methods. A nearby pipe close to the house produced a slow, steady drip. We put the method to the test by lying underneath the pipe and allowing the water to drip on our foreheads. This constant drip, we had heard, sent men mad and the thought of this accelerated our panic. We only lasted about 15 seconds before leaping up, terrified that we may have lost our sanity for all time.

In similar vein, we would find an overflowing rain gutter in one of the nearby works on Greenfield Road and stand underneath the torrent for ten minutes or so until we were both absolutely drenched through. When we got home, Mother said, "Oh my God, it has been raining, hasn't it," which amused us both no end.

Birthday parties were definitely 'home-made', improvising games and entertainment. Father would officiate as the 'judge' when the parlour was set up as a courtroom. We children were brought in one at a time and accused of various 'crimes'. We had to stand in front of the 'bench' with both our feet nervously on the black mat as sentence was passed on us. Whatever the sentence, it always ended with the words "down with the prisoner". This was the cue for the black mat to be whipped out from under our feet causing the prisoner to collapse in a heap. Mother stood by to make sure no heads were cracked on the floor.

Exploring further we found Turner Beck (Wanlass Water) and one day ventured up a pipe that went off in darkness but had water trickling out of it. It went on for a long way – hundreds of yards. We had to crawl, hunched up, but eventually the glimmer at the end became brighter and we found ourselves at the bottom of a very wide, very high shaft. There were step-irons up the side, so up we climbed, with a lot of difficulty where the step irons were missing or rusting away. Finally, we got to the top and found ourselves looking down into the water of the reservoir near the canal on Barrowford Road. We had climbed up those rickety and rotten iron steps up through the inside of the reservoir overflow shaft. There was no way down the outside, so it was back down the shaft and out along the tunnel. I guess we were very late home and in trouble again. However, by this age we knew we would be in double trouble if we told our parents exactly where we'd been.

David and I went to school together but I was not very studious or academically bright. Dyslexia wasn't recognised in those days, as such, but it certainly played a large part in giving me problems. At examination results time, I always searched for my name from the bottom of the list upwards and I didn't have to work up it very far.

Now, the family – on Father's side as well as on Mother's – had always been very well educated. Grandfather, Sagar Fort, sent all his children to private schools – the girls to finishing schools in France, Switzerland or London. He wanted his girls to be an attractive proposition as wives for professionals. Father was educated privately at Arnold House School in Blackpool. On leaving school, Father bought his first job as a secretary (yes, 'bought', for a fiver, to start in the office, as was customary at that time) – at Sough Bridge Mill. Even though Mother was also well educated, it was felt at the time that Father had married 'below his station' for some reason. There is a story that, on their wedding day, they ended up laying bricks but I know not why.

Mother continued with her belief in having a good education and was determined that Robert and I would be given the best chance

Left: Father (back row, second from the left) played rugby and soccer for the Colne first teams. Grandfather is on the back row, far right, in the bowler

of doing as well as we could. Robert was much brighter than I but we were both taken along to meet Dr. Foggerty at the other end of Colne for some private tuition to help get us through the eleven-plus examination, required at the time if we were to progress to the grammar school rather than a secondary modern technical school – this being the two-tier system in place before they were amalgamated into the current comprehensive schools system.

Dr. Foggerty didn't take on just anyone. We had to have an interview and he asked us both many questions. Robert was in his element and fluent with his answers. I was silent.

"Well, Mrs. Fort," said Foggerty, after a time of consideration, "I'll take the young one but I'm afraid I won't take the elder." So this rather defined my fate, as far as the family was concerned. I would end up in an honourable but manual trade, such as painter and decorator, postman or train station attendant, but my academic future looked pretty grim.

The actual eleven-plus examination was to be taken at Lord Street School, a little further into town. It's not surprising that I didn't do well. I journeyed there in fearful trepidation. Sitting down to start proceedings, I was a nervous wreck. A dyslexic is not at his best in an examination and, compounded by fear and nerves, the result was no surprise.

So Mother received a letter from the authorities saying that I had "... passed the examination to go to a secondary modern technical school..." which sounded good – until it was realised that it meant that I had failed to get through to grammar school.

Huggins did not pass the examination either. Of his three sisters, Cynthia went on to marry yet another who failed the eleven-plus – Police Constable John Stevens, later to become Lord Stevens after a wonderful career: he finally became Commissioner of the Metropolitan Police Force in London, the most senior police officer in the land. So we are in good company.

It was at about this time that, on top of all this educational stress, the whole family was thrown into a highly emotional change of circumstances and huge disruption by an aunt moving house.

Chapter 2

An Unpopular Move

Mother, Robert and I were all crying. We were having to leave Greenfield House Cottage and were travelling in the removal van on our way to Lancashire Ghyll, an old Fort family farmhouse.

The Forts had strong family ties in those days and always had. I still feel them, personally, although the modern Fort family is less strongly connected, I'm afraid. It is a loss in my opinion. The reason we were removing to Lancashire Ghyll was that Grandfather Sagar lived there with his youngest daughter but she was now moving out and getting married. So we were having to move in and look after him. It was our family responsibility.

Lancashire Ghyll was without electricity, sanitation or running water. We did have spring water, though. Water from the spring was piped to a tank and from there to the house. There was no mains water supply. The outside loo, the 'Thunderbox' was a shock. It was an earth closet, with a timber bench seat and two, yes, two holes for tandem occupation. Being joined by Grandfather, smoking his pipe, was definitely off-putting for a ten year old. The change from our comfortable existence in Greenfield House Cottage was dramatic. It was definitely a backward step in our opinion.

The house itself is situated in a magnificent location between Foulridge and Kelbrook on what was the old road to Skipton before the toll road was constructed down in the valley. I call it a road but it is only a narrow lane in dimensions. It has splendid views along the valley from Foulridge in the south towards Barnoldswick and Earby in the north. Across the valley, the purple, heather clad moorland of Weets Hill reaches 1300 feet above sea level. To its left, we could make out Pendle Hill in the middle distance towering even higher at over 1800 feet. It is often smothered in cloud, brought in on the westerly winds from the Irish Sea, condensing as they rise over the highest land in their path. The locals say that if you can see Pendle it is going to rain and if you can't see Pendle – it is raining. This damp climate was one of the key reasons that the textile industry was established in the area as the humidity facilitated the weaving of the cotton yarn into cloth.

It was only later in life that I grew to appreciate the wonderful countryside. At the time of the move, I was much more concerned with day-to-day existence and the loss of amenities and home comforts that we had suffered.

Below: Grandfather, Sagar Fort, outside Lancashire Ghyll with his 'muck' cart used to carry fertiliser to the vegetable garden

Above: Lancashire Ghyll is the building with the white gable end. Just above it is the 'Old House' and Higher Hague Farm is at the very top edge of the photograph

Below: The lathe bought by Mother on Colne market for my 14th birthday

Behind the house and slightly uphill was the old farmhouse or what we called the 'Old House'. No longer occupied it was, originally, an older style farmhouse with the attached barn built as an extension to the house. This was where we stored implements and, later, my first lathe, bought by Mother as a 14th birthday present for £14.0s.0d (about £400 in today's value) on Colne market.

The Old House was where we had the big old copper to do the laundry. The copper sat over an open fire to heat the water. Washing powder was added and the clothes dropped into the hot water, near to boiling. A posser was used to beat and agitate the clothes to dislodge the grime and grit for half an hour, or so. The posser had a long wooden shaft, broomstick-like, with a perforated, copper plunger at one end – an inverted bowl-shape bordered with perforations – and a tee-bar handle at the other to aid rotation. After rinsing in clean water, the clothes were fed between the two rollers of a hand-cranked mangle, which removed the excess water prior to pegging out on a washing line. I mention these details to fully illustrate the primitive conditions in which we, brother Robert and I, were growing up. This was the norm: no luxuries, no washing machine, no electricity, candles to go to bed with, paraffin lamps to read by, a range to cook on – tough but coped with. It was what we were used to – or became used to, as we had electricity at Greenfield House.

Slightly below our house, and just across the road, was another farm looking after the fields stretching down towards the valley bottom. The farmer occupant, Harry Simpson, is still there today and still selling his meat to a local butcher in Barnoldswick. His beef is excellent, reputedly.

The move to Lancashire Ghyll brought us much nearer to the Fort family roots. Our family can be traced back to Richarde Forte who lived at Acornlea Hall, only a couple of fields away, and he married Jennet Kirke in 1730. We were also nearer to the village of Kelbrook, one mile down the lane, which was a centre of the family's commercial activity.

Extracting stone from the quarry at Salterforth, Great-Grandfather Robert Fort had built many houses in Kelbrook. The Forts then owned 49 houses in the village, including five farms, two shops, all of Main Street and the slaughterhouse. Perhaps this spirit of enterprise has survived genetically in some way to explain my commercial success. It has certainly created a lasting impression on me as I can recount in detail a lot of the business activities of those days.

Land owned by us was rented out at a 'peppercorn' rent but on a short, twelve-month lease. This was to maintain the ability to evict the tenant at short notice. If a new house was built which overlooked an existing house, then a 'window light' rent was payable to the existing house owner – invariably, the Forts. Rent from window light was two shillings and sixpence per year, per house.

As well as these local properties, we also had houses in Foulridge, Earby and Colne. On Fridays, rent collection day, the men folk of the family would link up in pairs to collect rent from the rougher areas of Colne, such as Waterside in the South Valley – an area so run-down that a lot of the housing was demolished in the nineteen-thirties. The house would be entered without knocking at the door and the week's

Above: A 'posser' used on wash day

Left: Acornlea Hall, Foulridge, home of the Forts in the 18th Century

rent demanded with no civility at all. A good walking stick was carried and used end-on to the chest of anyone approaching in a threatening manner. Grandfather demonstrated the technique to me and on me – it is very effective. The table at Lancashire Ghyll, I remember, used to be full of pound notes on rent day. The family did not benefit much at all from rent as most of it went in tax.

In spite of all the family assets, we were not wealthy in cash terms: we all lived like church mice. The most important thing of all, which was drummed into us frequently, was not to spend any money. Now, that part of our genetic make-up was not passed down to me.

Although honouring this frugal philosophy, money was forthcoming for education. This was recognition of its importance in the family, which was not terribly common locally at that time and certainly not affordable to all but the very well off. All four children of Grandfather Sagar were put through private education, as mentioned before. This was to enable the girls to be better provided for by marrying into the professions as well as to make Father best prepared for commercial life.

Grandfather Sagar Fort, our new house mate, had retired at the very young age of 42 after inheriting from his father. He was the oldest male offspring so he collected the entire estate. When his father, Great-Grandfather Robert Fort, died, he had left significant wealth and property built up by the hard work of his and previous generations. It was Robert himself who was recognised as being the successful local entrepreneur of the day and he was well respected. He sat on various committees and, in 1898, was on the original board of directors of the Kelbrook Mill Company who owned the local Sough Bridge Mill

Right: Grandfather hauling 'muck' on Skipton Old Road, long before the family moved to Lancashire Ghyll

housing around 500 looms. To this day, the family still owns 15% of the Company.

There were many heated discussions regarding the general meetings of the Kelbrook Mill Company. Grandfather and Father would be complaining bitterly about the shareholders who were demanding this or that, complaining about directors' fees or the dividends, and would curse them most vehemently. Shareholders, it seemed, did not know what they were talking about and, simply, they were a nuisance.

Growing up in this atmosphere of boardroom level politics caused attitudes and opinions to be rubbed off onto me to some measure. At the age of ten or twelve I already had planted in my mind that running a private company was the thing to do and going public with shareholders was to be avoided.

It is apparent, therefore, that there was a wide range of activities in which the family was involved and that contributed to the family estate. The assets created had become significant and were carefully preserved. Day to day life would never reveal the considerable accumulation of wealth by extravagant levels of spending. We would never buy anything other than absolute essentials.

The family was thrown into turmoil and a terrible dispute over the inheritance of the estate on the death of Grandfather. My father and his three sisters contested the inheritance for twenty-one years. The arguments were not settled until all the surviving members of that generation had passed on.

On my mother's side of the family, things were not always as financially secure. Her father, Edward Bury, was in the textile business but, unfortunately, was bankrupt twice in his career.

Robert and I were still at school in Colne. When we needed to travel into town, we would walk down through the long grass to the main road a couple of fields away in our wellingtons, carrying shoes. The wellies would be left under the stile for our return as we changed into shoes for the bus ride into town. We became very used to this and the wellies were always there when we got back. I wonder if the same would be true today?

It was via this route that I travelled each weekday to Primet Secondary Modern School, a journey of some three and a half miles. Secondary school started to make more sense over time and I found that I was getting more out of schooling than I ever did at primary school. Materials were still in short supply so a lack of wood for woodwork class limited us to making a very small book rack. At least it was hands-on and creative – I had made something myself. That was where I gained most satisfaction.

After a few years, I started to look for my name on the examination

Above: Evidence of the Fort family house building activities in Kelbrook

results list from the top downwards instead of from the bottom up, as previously. Finally I would find myself above halfway. Progress.

I was made a prefect – the first taste of having some sort of authority. I didn't know why they made me a prefect. I had never thought that I might be made one but at least I was now, somehow, picked out as an individual rather than remaining simply as one of the herd. It made me think that perhaps I could get somewhere in life other than be pigeonholed as one destined not to get very far.

I also managed to make the school team both for football and cricket – perhaps inheriting some sporting gene from my father who had played soccer and rugby for the Colne first team.

Father was still working away at the mill on Clarence Street with his two business partners, Harry Carey and William Smith. The company had grown to employ between fifty and a hundred people. I used to work there on the occasional Saturday morning for sixpence doing odd jobs around the place. Rules for employees were strict. If a worker turned up late at the mill, management would tell him that he wasn't required that day and he would lose the day's pay.

Commission weaving at the mill was weaving to order for customers in Manchester, mainly made up of the Jewish textile merchants. They were a tough bunch and if there was the slightest fault in the cloth, the whole batch was rejected and returned – not always quite fairly in Father's view.

Still, the mill made good profits, so it was a terrible shock when the Freeholder of the mill, Whittaker, would not renew the lease and demanded the property back. Father was irate that he could be treated

in this way: he could have 'murdered' Whittaker. Another lesson learned – always buy freehold, never leasehold.

Father was out of work. There was no unemployment benefit then, of course, and he was in a complete whirl for six months before finding work again in his old profession as a tackler – firstly at what became the Bairdtex Mill in Trawden (later Michael Bannister's mill) and then Fernbank Mill in Barnoldswick. Fernbank Road in Barnoldswick was where Uncle Phillip lived, too.

We weren't going to starve, though. The make do and mend philosophy continued to guide our lives. Grandfather, I remember, was forever giving Robert and me jobs around the house and garden. He grew vegetables – had done all his life – and we were drummed into tending the crops. He, with Father, also grew tobacco plants and made his own pipe tobacco up in the Old House They both had old wooden pipes and Robert and I made one for ourselves, drilling out a pipe stem and assembling it with a crude bowl. Smoking was not very appealing to me at all but Robert, I'm afraid, took to it later and smoked a pipe for many years. I am convinced it was a factor in his early demise.

I had started to keep hens, buying a few Bantams initially from Oswaldtwistle market. Eventually I had built up the flock to 70 Rhode Island Reds, which laid bigger eggs than Bantams, and the Milk Marketing Board would call each week to collect the eggs. I managed to earn a good bit of spending money this way, especially as Mother paid for the feed and I kept all the money from selling the eggs. This was probably the earliest indication of a canny operator. I still have the balance sheet and expenditure notes from this early commercial

*Right and opposite:
Extract from my egg
business accounts*

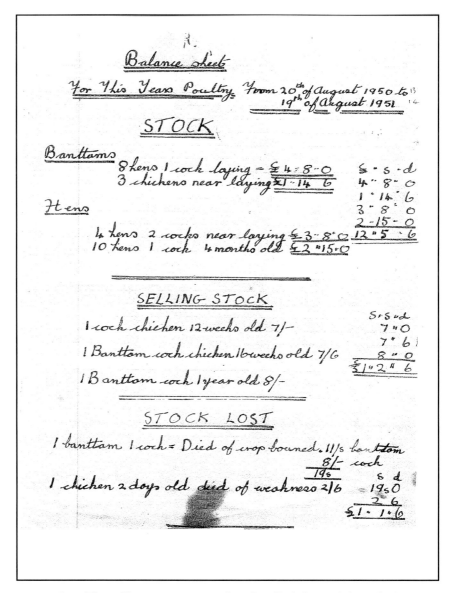

A.

Balance sheet

For This Years Poultry From 20th of August 1950 to
19th of August 1951

STOCK

Banttams

			£ - s - d
8 hens 1 cock laying	= £ 4 - 8 - 0		4 - 8 - 0
3 chickens near laying	£ 1 - 14 - 6		1 - 14 - 6

Hens

			3 - 8 - 0
4 hens 2 cocks near laying	£ 3 - 8 - 0		2 - 15 - 0
10 hens 1 cock 4 months old	£ 2 - 15 - 0		12 - 5 - 6

SELLING STOCK

	s - s - d
1 cock chicken 12 weeks old 7/-	7 - 0
1 Banttam cock chicken 16 weeks old 7/6	7 - 6
1 Banttam cock 1 year old 8/-	8 - 0
	£ 1 - 2 - 6

STOCK LOST

1 banttam 1 cock = Died of crop bouned. 11/s banttam

8/- cock

19s

	s d
1 chicken 2 days old died of weakness 2/6	= 19s 0
	2 - 6
	£ 1 - 1 - 6

enterprise. They illustrate an eye for detailed financial analysis at an early age, at 13 years old, – if not tremendous profits. My problem with dyslexia did not affect this numerical exercise and I found that, more and more, I was able to cope with the complaint at school – or, at least, find a way around any issues. Numerical problems were fine – it was words with which I struggled.

David Huggins had also failed his eleven-plus examination but gone away to a private school in Durham. Brother Robert had passed following individual, private tuition to make sure he made it to grammar school. David and I remained firm friends and would get together for various adventures. One time we looked up in the library

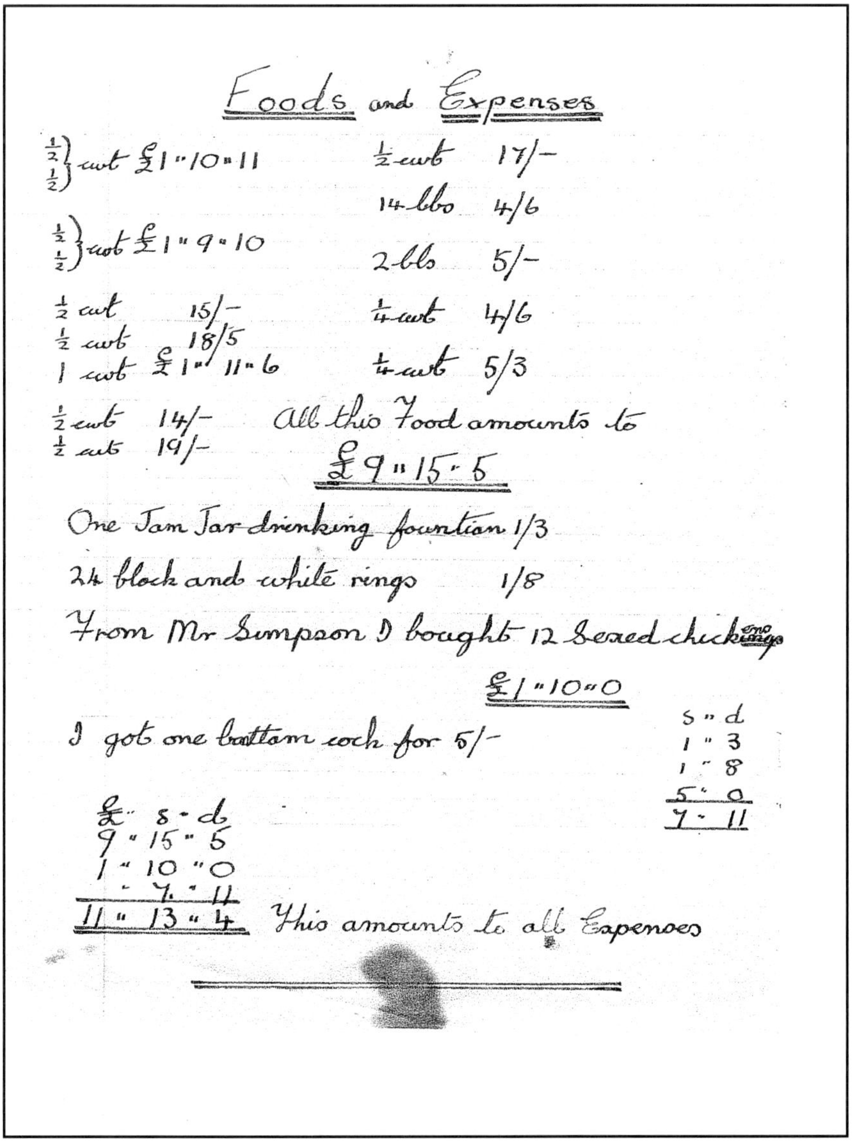

<u>Foods</u> and <u>Expenses</u>

½ ½ } cwt £1"10"11	½ cwt	17/-
	14 lbs	4/6
½ ½ } cwt £1"9"10	2 lbs	5/-
½ cwt 15/-	¼ cwt	4/6
½ cwt 18/5		
1 cwt £1"11"6	¼ cwt	5/3
½ cwt 14/-	All this Food amounts to	
½ cwt 19/-		

<u>£9"15"5</u>

One Jam Jar drinking fountian 1/3

24 black and white rings   1/8

From Mr Simpson I bought 12 Sexed chickens

<u>£1"10"0</u>

I got one battam cock for 5/-

```
                              s " d
                              1 " 3
                              1 " 8
                              5 " 0
                              7 " 11
   £ " s " d
   9 " 15 " 5
   1 " 10 " 0
   -  " 7 " 11
  11 " 13 " 4   This amounts to all Expenses
```

how to manufacture gunpowder. We had to buy each component powder from three different shops otherwise the shopkeeper would realise what we were up to and refuse to let us have them. We managed to obtain what was required and had a happy time blowing large holes in the countryside – well, dustbin lid size was as large to us as a bomb crater. Luckily, we survived the manufacturing process that could have gone so horribly wrong very easily.

David's father, the vicar, used to take the Huggins family on holiday to Silecroft, near Ulverston, on the west coast. They would take me too and I could be there for several weeks in the tent that Mother had made for me. Once I had to travel there alone, on the train, with my

*Right: The family
looking very smart
when we are invited
out to friends for tea*

bicycle. That was a rather tortuous expedition but I got there in the end. They were great times – playing on the beach and I remember making a crude raft on the beach with David and attempting to put to sea: a maiden nautical adventure. I wonder if that is what first gave me the taste for waterborne sport?

Much later, I was to have a more serious attempt with friend and fellow apprentice, David Fleetwood. We travelled by train to Fairhaven Lake at St. Anne's on Sea. It was possible to hire a sailing dinghy there from a man in a hut by the shore. On the hut was a sign stating that "This could be you" and showing an upturned dinghy with would-be sailors struggling in the water – an ominous picture. "So you're sure you lads can sail?" the man asked. "Oh, yes, we've sailed before," we lied. Again we survived but, more critically, we loved it – under sail on the water – fantastic. I had no idea at the time, of course, but these watery adventures set my course in life in so many ways. We talk of pivotal moments in life and I've mentioned how influential they can be: this was to be one of the most life defining of all.

Coincidence, too, crops up again here. Many years later I met Graham Murray at Royal Windermere Yacht Club when we both sailed the same class of boat, the Soling. Later, Graham crewed for me in my boats and we have had many, many sailing races together over the years. Graham's first sailing experience was also on the water at Fairhaven Lake – and not only on but in the water, as it turned out. Graham was sailing with his father. Father was in charge and thought he was doing well. Graham was not at all convinced and was so worried that he jumped ship to swim ashore. He was a strong swimmer and thought

he had a better chance of survival by swimming ashore rather than staying with the boat – possibly going down with all hands. Graham first sailed there in 1958 at the age of ten and I just two years earlier in 1956, aged 19 years.

The playful days of school were drawing to a close and I was approaching the time to leave school for good. My academic achievements were not encouraging when it came to career choice. Options before me included postman, painter and decorator or tinsmith – not very appealing and, however suitable for others of an appropriate persuasion, they weren't for me. But did I have a choice? It looked bleak.

Mother had other ideas.

Chapter 3

Engineering a Career

Mother, as ever, was doing her best for her offspring. She was pulling out all the stops to make sure that I had the best opportunity of a reasonable career – even for me, the son less likely to prosper – as it seemed at the time. I wasn't making any meaningful decisions at the age of 15 years let alone plotting a career path, I was simply doing as I was told and following on. I had no real idea of careers and progress – of doing well in life. I couldn't see ahead much further than the hens. It was only much later in life that I appreciated just how much thought and effort had gone into giving me direction.

Uncle McIntyre worked at the Rolls Royce factory in Barnoldswick – at the Bankfield site. He was married to Father's sister, Lucy. We called him by his surname to avoid confusion as we already had an Uncle Robert. Although I'm unsure on this, I think there must have been some behind-the-scenes arrangements and influences involved as I managed to be listed as a candidate for a prestigious apprenticeship at the company. For a schoolboy of modest academic achievement to be included, it must have been the case.

The catchment area for applications stretched as far as Skipton and

Ilkley in Yorkshire and to Burnley in Lancashire. There was an intake of 90 apprentices that year, mainly from grammar schools. At the time, the factory employed 4,500 people making military engines. (Currently, in our own company, Fort Vale Engineering, by comparison, we employ around 400 at our manufacturing centre in Lancashire and our yearly intake of new apprentices is 8 or so, which is 2% of the total workforce – exactly the same ratio as at Rolls Royce when I joined.)

Mother took me along to the factory at Bankfield for my interview. She saw me through to the gatehouse (which is still there, by the way) before leaving.

The interview was pretty detailed: I was asked many questions. I was quizzed on the conversion of fractions into decimals. The interviewer started with the easy and, supposedly obvious, "Can you tell me what half an inch is in decimals?" he asked.

It can't be this easy, I thought as I answered, "Nought point five, sir."

"And a quarter?" he continued.

"Nought point two five, sir" and I continued with the correct answers as he lowered the fraction further.

Fortunately, I knew the decimal conversions by heart. He got to "One thirty-second?" and when he reached "One sixty-fourth?" and I answered correctly, "Nought point nought one five six two five, sir," he stopped. Thinking back, that must have been pretty impressive from a fifteen year old. It was figures, you see, not words so I could cope. I was caught out on one point, however, as I did not know what a micrometer was.

I did pass the interview and was accepted as a Rolls Royce apprentice. These were exciting days at Rolls Royce and I really do consider myself to be very lucky in being a young man at this period in history. It was ten years previously, in 1942, that Sir Frank Whittle had contracted Rolls to produce their first jet engine, the WR1, and only eight years

Below left: The Gloster Meteor jet fighter

Below right: Sir Frank Whittle, pioneering engineer of the jet engine

earlier that their first production engine, the 'Welland', powered the Gloster Meteor jet fighter – a terrific aircraft.

German engineers had the basic design much earlier and had recognised the potential when the Whittle registered patent of 1930 gave the details away. The British government of the time did not recognise the potential and had failed to list it as 'Secret', which would have kept the design under wraps.

As I joined the company in 1952 the Cold War was starting to bite and we had already given our jet engine technology, together with some actual engines, to our wartime allies, the Americans and the Russians, who successfully re-engineered the supplied engines for their own aircraft. We had surrendered our hard-earned technical knowledge and also our commercial advantage not only to the enemy but to an eventual competitor and to a potential future enemy. It was a decision born at the time from the fear of losing the war but it has been questioned since.

The task for Rolls Royce was to stay ahead of the game. Development was the key. The industry and the technology were advancing rapidly. To join the Company at this stage in its life was a tremendous buzz: there was so much going on and to a young lad it was fascinating.

I started work in the Assembly Drawing Office. It was probably the best area, for me in particular, out of all the departments and I wonder if Uncle McIntyre had something to do with this happy outcome too. It was a place where I could see for the first time that the power of the pencil could magic-up real things – components and products which could actually be made.

One unnerving episode that startled me on my first arrival was seeing on the office door a sign saying ASSY DO. It stood, of course, for Assembly Drawing Office but being dyslexic I read it in my haste as ESSAY DO. That scared the daylights out of me as I thought it was a room where I must DO an ESSAY and that it was my turn next. I thought I'd left all that behind at school. They must have discovered my poor level of English and it was another test I had to complete was my mistaken assumption.

Mr. Les Sayer, under whom we were working, was then number two in command of the whole of the Rolls Royce factory, such was the importance of the department. All the latest engine advancements were designed and developed here. As I was under 16 years at the time, I was not allowed to work any machines – those were the rules. So, for the first nine months of my time there, I was sent to get drawings, deliver messages and run errands, which sent me all over the place. I enjoyed that. Every drawing had a number six digits long and up to half a dozen of these drawing numbers were read out to me when I was to fetch drawings from the filing cabinets. If I forgot one number and had to ask for it again I was in big trouble. (It's strange what sticks in the mind after all these years.) But I got very capable at remembering them – numbers again, you see. There were at least three or four manned drawing boards in the office and I was the 'tea-boy'.

I also had to take phone calls in the period between 7.30 a.m. when I started work and 9.00 a.m. when the more senior staff arrived. I hated that bit – we had no telephone at home so I was totally unused to this daunting operation. I was never comfortable on the telephone and am still not.

One positive result of my early duties is my ability to file documents well. I had to file away letters that came into the office and woe betide me if I got one wrong. This discipline of correct filing was very important and it is because it was drummed into me so forcefully that I still insist on similar accuracy in my offices now. Only recently I managed to retrieve easily the original, first-year financial accounts from the start up of my business in 1967.

Being used to a school timetable, the hours at work were long and took some getting used to. My school day started at 9.00 a.m. so starting work at 7.30 a.m. was hard. I had to get up at 6.00 a.m., have breakfast and catch a bus on the main road two fields away. The bus ride took half an hour. Most of the workers there travelled in by bus. Cars were not common in the early fifties. Senior staff, as opposed to shop floor workers, started at 9.00 a.m. After a full days work I did not get back home until 6.00 p.m. At 15 years of age, it was quite an ordeal and a huge change. I was exhausted. It was during this period, however, that I really started to notice the green fields; the countryside as a whole and I appreciated the rural surroundings of home.

Right: My actual apprenticeship certificate

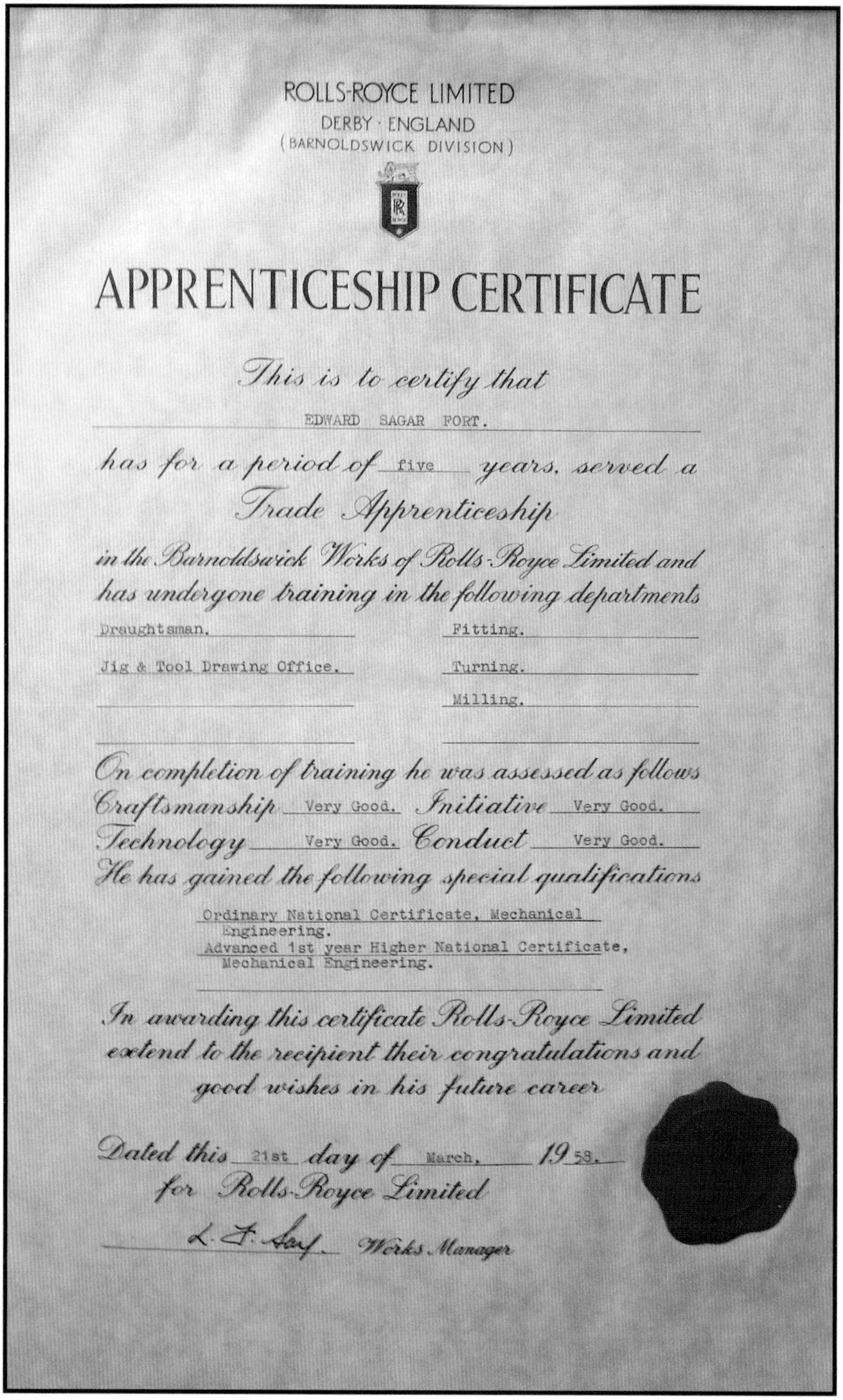

ROLLS-ROYCE LIMITED
DERBY · ENGLAND
(BARNOLDSWICK DIVISION)

APPRENTICESHIP CERTIFICATE

This is to certify that

EDWARD SAGAR FORT.

has for a period of five years, served a

Trade Apprenticeship

in the Barnoldswick Works of Rolls-Royce Limited and has undergone training in the following departments

Draughtsman. Fitting.

Jig & Tool Drawing Office. Turning.

Milling.

On completion of training he was assessed as follows

Craftsmanship Very Good. Initiative Very Good.

Technology Very Good. Conduct Very Good.

He has gained the following special qualifications

Ordinary National Certificate, Mechanical Engineering.
Advanced 1st year Higher National Certificate, Mechanical Engineering.

In awarding this certificate Rolls-Royce Limited extend to the recipient their congratulations and good wishes in his future career

Dated this 21st day of March, 1958.

for Rolls-Royce Limited

L. F. Hay Works Manager

It was at this time that I had one of what I term my 'near death experiences'. Rolls Royce arranged, very generously, an annual trip to take some apprentices to the Farnborough Airshow. This was much

Left: I am the apprentice on the far left, on the Rolls Royce float in a parade, passing Kelbrook village. The row of houses in the background was built by Great-Grandfather

appreciated by all who went. We travelled down by bus, or 'charabanc' as we called them, with a few Rolls employees too. Following the airshow, the party would go up to London and see a concert before travelling back to Lancashire very late at night, totally worn out.

While at the airshow, during a display of the de Havilland DH110 prototype jet fighter, the aircraft broke up. The two engines broke free and one flew over my head. It happened so quickly that it did not register that this was not actually part of the demonstration until the engine hurtled into the watching spectators behind me. Several pieces of the plane ploughed into the crowd. Thirty-one people died, including the two aircrew, pilot John Derry and his flight test observer, Anthony Richards. I was standing not far away from the carnage. It is a traumatic memory, which is hard to forget. It was the 6th of September, 1952.

I was still young and David Huggins and I still had lads' adventures. We had always competed in a 'who has the best bike' competition, leapfrogging each other, but by now we had comparable machines, with derailleur gears too. Our excursions took us to the old, abandoned shooting lodge, high on the moors above Kelbrook, where we explored the woods and swam in the icy waters of the lake.

My constructive nature, together with the experience of working at Rolls Royce, prompted some research into jet engines. I decided it would be quite feasible to put together a ramjet type of engine. I drew the parts, made them all and assembled the prototype for a test run. Ramjets need a high velocity airflow to initiate combustion of the paraffin fuel, so Huggins was called for. Standing him on the top of a stone wall next to the midden, I instructed him to swing round the engine mounted at the end of a long piece of string, at high speed, whilst I observed for analysis. It did not work. I blamed Huggins, of course, whom I accused of being frightened by the possibility of falling into the midden and not trying hard enough.

If I cycled to work, as I did later, I could save 6d a journey (about 70p in today's value) or a whole pound for every 40 trips.

In the Drawing Office I was occasionally allowed to design and draw a simple component – this was the power of the pencil now in my own hands. Wonderful. Also, I was beginning to realize the importance of education and that if I didn't get my head down and focus on passing examinations then I would not progress. I might become proficient working on production machines in the machine shop but I would not be able to advance into design and development, which was where I really wanted to be.

I started at night school in September 1952 at the very bottom of the ladder. Most of my colleagues there were from the Grammar Schools. The course was in stages – T1, S1 and S2 as I recall. It was hard but Mother, again, was supportive and encouraging. I was given 16 shillings a week pocket money (about £20 today) whilst attending the course. My parents helped me to catch up, providing private tuition after work so that I could get closer to the level of the Grammar School boys.

I enjoyed attending Nelson and Colne Technical College – they had a steam engine. In those days, steam turbine engines were used on ships so I began to learn about super heated steam and related technology. I started S2 examinations in Year 3 and was ecstatic when I came out in second place in class. This was a real achievement after what seemed to have been a long, uphill slog. We had an impressive presentation evening at the Imperial Ballroom in Nelson and I was very proud to receive a prize: a small slide rule, which I treasured and still have in my office drawer today.

Encouraged by success and realizing that I could go further with effort and commitment, in spite of having been unpromising at school, I set my sights higher.

I decided to try for my HND and went to Burnley College. When I had completed the first year of this course, the college introduced an HND sandwich course. This was a better course for me, more suited to my way of learning. The sandwich element included six months in industry, which I could take at Rolls Royce, then six months at college. The company were not keen on this new type of course and they wanted me to stay on in full time production work but I decided to go ahead in any case. What was really excellent during my time at Rolls was that each of the six month periods were spent in a different department. This broadened my experience tremendously.

Each department Foreman or Charge Hand kept a close eye on me to ascertain my capabilities at every step.

It turned out that my skills in setting and operating the machine tools were not great. This was probably for the best as those who were recognised as being particularly talented in that area and who became top, skilled machine operators were moved invariably to the jig boring section for the remainder of their working life. That would not have been a direction for me. It would have denied my design ambitions.

Back at college, it was put to me in no uncertain terms by the college principal, Dr. Rifkin, that I had only just made it onto the course. I would have to work hard, he said. He was, of course, absolutely correct and I realized that I had pushed my learning abilities to the limit by aiming for this HND course. Studies would include extremely taxing subjects such as higher level mathematics and stress analysis, which were very much above my level.

During the course, a gentleman from a local company that supplied equipment to the hairdressing profession approached the college. He needed someone to work on a project to detail components for a hair dryer. The project was offered to all students and I was fortunate enough to win the work.

I had to carry out the project at home, which was difficult in so far as we had no electricity and I had no drawing board there. Working at night under the light of an Aladdin paraffin lamp on the breakfast table, I was kept busy until all hours drawing the components in pen and ink on Irish linen – the medium used for technical drawings then. It was my first experience of working for a customer.

Back at Rolls Royce, once having attained my ONC, I graduated to the Apprentice Draughtsman Training School in the Jig and Tool Drawing Office. This was a six month course where only the top two of six apprentices training would qualify to be placed and work in the Jig and Tool Drawing Office at the end of the course. It was another tough time needing commitment and focus. My tutor, John Pullen, once had to say to me, "Look here, Fort, unless you pull your finger out you are going back to the shop floor." Another kick in the pants – another realisation that hard work was needed to progress in life.

At the end of the course I managed to do well in the examination and began working in the Jig and Tool Drawing Office. This was split into various sections, each with a section leader who kept a very close eye on work and would not tolerate the slightest mistake. We used a manual cylindrical calculator (only found in a museum now) or log tables for working out the various angles on the grinding fixtures.

These were days of amassing experience. Life's learning curve was not restricted to engineering technicalities. Behaviour in the works, and particularly on the shop floor, had a traditional set of rules. Step

Below: The paraffin lamp I used for illumination during the drawing of hair dryer components at Lancashire Ghyll in the absence of electricity

out of line – a very thin line – and one was very quickly and firmly knocked back to within the acceptable limits. Within those limits the camaraderie, help and encouragement were striking and sincere. The older workers were always ready to help and advise those learning. They remembered how hard it was when first starting work – and we certainly needed all the help we could get. They were a close-knit band of warriors always ready to help each other out – but don't cross that line.

Rolls Royce had a well-structured and respected hierarchical class system. One always addressed section leaders as 'Mister So-and-so' and with a 'Yes, Sir' or 'No, Sir' when replying to questions. There were five canteens, ranked at different staff levels with the highest being for top management and VIPs. It had waiter service. Over the whole nine years that I worked there, I never progressed up the ladder beyond the fifth, the lowest level canteen.

These were also days of earning an income. Earning money had been something new when first starting work, of course, but it felt strange to collect money in a little brown envelope every week. It was strange but made one feel part of the adult world at last and gave a limited degree of independence. It was my money, earned by me and not simply given as spending money from a parent. To begin with I earned one pound and ten shillings a week (£1.10s.0d – in old money or £40 today).

A skilled tradesman at the time would be earning £11.4s.6d (£283 today) a week. The standard working week was 48 hours and most factories also worked the Saturday morning. Holidays were only Bank

Right: Rolls Royce, Ghyll Brow Plant, where I went to work on jet engine turbine blades

Holidays plus one week – traditionally called 'Wakes Week'. This one week stemmed from the textile industry when the mill would be shut down for one complete week for all the maintenance to be done. Clocking in late for work by more than three minutes resulted in one being 'quartered', which is losing a quarter of an hour's pay. Repeat offences resulted in a serious rebuke at salary review time.

I could increase my earnings significantly by working overtime hours. This was important to me and I would try to impress the section leader, Neville Crowson, and obtain the most overtime possible. He came around every Monday morning to ask what overtime you could work that week. You could work Tuesday evening, Thursday evening and Saturday morning and if you did all three you were then allowed to work Sunday. I would always try to do all this overtime. Overtime during the week paid time-and-a-third; Saturdays paid time-and-a-half but Sundays, if you could get work on a Sunday at all, paid double time. The Fort family character I had in me prompted a pursuit of maximum possible income.

I had a bit of an interest in the stock market at the time and this was encouraged when I saw a competition in the Daily Mail one day. It was a virtual investment competition starting with a fictional one thousand pounds. I played the game without actually sending in an entry. At the end of the competition, I found that I had come very close to the winning score.

So, at the age of 19, I asked Father if he knew of any stockbrokers. He found a small stockbroker in Colne, a Mr. Leeming, and I invested the princely sum of £125.0s.0d (about £2,800 today) in my first stock holdings. I picked four mainstream companies – British Steel was one, although I forget which the others were. Leeming asked Father where his son was getting these big ideas at his age. I have invested in shares ever since, building a sizeable portfolio over time.

Passing the HND examination and being awarded with the diploma gave me a psychological boost after a huge sigh of relief. I had not been confident at all of getting through. Taking the news of success back to the bosses at Rolls Royce was an opportunity to push for moving on and moving up.

I was working under Jim Ratcliffe, Head of the Jig and Tool Drawing Office, overseeing some hundred or so employees. I said to him one day, full of the success of my new qualification, "Look here, Mr. Ratcliffe, I want a better job than working in this drawing office, particularly now that I have my HND." He looked at me rather aghast, as he was not usually addressed in such a manner.

Shortly afterwards, although I was not to know how or why, I was moved from the Jig and Tool Drawing Office at Bankfield to the Ghyll Brow plant, a separate and more modern site situated further up the road towards Skipton by a mile or so where they specialised in forging the low- and high-pressure turbine blades, the first stage of manufacturing the turbines. At Ghyll Brow I became assistant to the Press Shop Superintendant, George Eccles. (As I write this in 2016, the workforce at Rolls has been cut back and Fort Vale Engineering at Simonstone now employs more than the Ghyll Bank plant where I finished my apprenticeship.)

I continued to design and detail components – with highly complex drawings by this time. I was proud of the skills learnt and the professional level of accuracy I was able to achieve in the drawings. Eventually I progressed to working on the technical side of producing turbine blades.

Turbine blades in the combustion chamber of a jet engine are subject to extremely high temperatures. Today they are manufactured in exotic materials by advanced casting techniques controlling the alignment of the crystal structure of the material for strength. They have to be cooled to be efficient in the power they produce and the operating temperatures reached can be higher than the actual melting point of the materials used in some cases. So they are cast with a carefully designed hole pattern running through the blade through which to pass cooling air.

Back to my days at Rolls. The turbine blades we produced in those days were forged not cast and they, too, needed cooling. I was responsible for ensuring that we put the holes through the forgings correctly. The work was very innovative but hard. It was a long slog but I really enjoyed the task and achieving significant results. It took me between six and nine months to develop an efficient hole pattern but it was fundamental to the engine power output. Efficient cooling of our turbine blades increased the power output of the engine by 50%. I often thought that if the Russians had got hold of me at that time, I would have been quite a catch as I could have been put to work increasing the power output of their engines too.

I was working at the time with two other men in the office – Peter Jennings and Geoff Holt. We got on well together. There was always plenty of banter and at the end of the week when we collected our pay packets, we might bet each other on some trivial, spur of the moment challenge. One thing we also did, pretty well as a habit each week, was to scan the Situations Vacant columns of the local newspaper. An advertisement was spotted for a position at Lucas Aerospace in Burnley. It was for a Junior Combustion Engineer. We jokingly discussed how we might be suitable for the post with the related work we were doing at Rolls Royce. The subject of the weekly bet arose.

"You keep talking about moving jobs, Fort," said Peter, "but I will bet you won't apply for this job at Lucas!" and so 7/6d (about £14 today) was laid that I would not apply for the job.

It was for a laugh and as a joke again that I applied. (Years later, in similar vein, it was the joke offer for two old machines in Yeadon that got me into trouble.) I won the bet. After attending an interview I was given the job and left Rolls Royce after eight years there to start with Lucas at Wood Top Works in Burnley. I was 23 years old.

Lucas was actually a major supplier to Rolls, supplying spare flame tubes and fuel systems for the Rolls Royce jet engines. When I was leaving, the Personnel Officer said to me, "Had the Managing Director [of Rolls Royce – Les Sayer] known you were going to join Lucas, he would have made sure you didn't get the job" – by which he meant that pressure would have been put on the management at Lucas to deny me the post. Les Sayer knew me from my time in the Assembly Drawing Office, had followed my progress through the company and had me marked as a star apprentice – but he was away or tied up at the crucial time of my leaving and missed the opportunity to prevent my departure.

One of my early projects at Lucas was nothing to do with jet engines at all – although it was still concerning combustion. Some oil-fired heaters on railway carriages were failing and it was not known just why they were. We set up a test rig with reverse heat pumps to drop the ambient temperature to winter levels and ran the heaters over several months, eight hours on, eight hours off. I proved conclusively that it was a poor design of combustion chamber that was causing the failures. This was escalated by toffee wrappers and other rubbish from the station platforms being sucked into the air intake, restricting the airflow and altering the air-to-fuel ratio. I was so pleased with myself at this result that I threatened to write to the Chairman in Birmingham, Oliver Lucas, regarding the tests: swanking again, I suppose. I was threatened with being "sent to Coventry" if I did write the letter so I abandoned that idea.

I was involved in many of the test rigs concerning flow rates at Lucas. I would design and create the drawings for the rigs, complete the testing and write up the reports. I hated writing the long, detailed reports – the fact that they needed more words than numbers creating issues for me again. It would take me two or three times longer to write the meticulous reports than to do the whole of the test itself. The experience with these test rigs – their design, operation and the flow instrumentation – was later to become crucial in the development of pressure relief valves at Fort Vale. The high standards achieved at Lucas were reflected in the advanced designs and superior performance that revolutionised the safety relief valves that Fort Vale manufactured for the road and rail transport industry. We outperformed all the competition by a considerable margin.

Later at Lucas, I worked on the Rover Rotax starter motor engine that powered up the Rolls Royce Pegasus engine used on the Harrier jump jet. The Harrier brought a new dimension to the flexibility of aerial operations with its vertical take-off capability and brought about the shorter, ski-jump aircraft carriers. It is no longer in RAF squadrons, sadly, being retired in 2010, although variants are still in service in the United States.

The project was very interesting indeed. We used the gas turbine engine running at 46,000 rpm developing 120 bhp. Our team made the spares and the angular combustion chamber that was used to carry out all the high altitude tests. These provided the conditions of very low temperatures (-40°C) and thin atmosphere. We were testing to ensure that there were no hot spots in the combustion chamber at altitude. I concentrated on the rig work and temperature traverses, working on the sprayers.

A high altitude test rig had been brought to Burnley, to Lucas back in the UK, from Germany during the repatriation period as the Second World War loomed. Other cutting-edge projects underway at Lucas at the time included work on the flame tubes for the Concorde engines, the Bristol Olympic 596, and the TSR2 purging systems, the former a success in its day – the latter cancelled by government before it could be produced for service (although a prototype did fly).

Whilst I was working at Lucas, a lot of graduates joined the company from university. They were horrified that (a) I could do the highly technical job without being a university graduate and (b) I knew all about manufacturing. Of course they had no industry experience whereas I had been working with the shop floor for over eight years. I had been involved with the manufacturing process from the age of 15 years. Some were disillusioned and left to get a higher degree so they could leap frog people like Ted Fort.

After three years at Lucas Aerospace, I resigned and went sailing.

Chapter 4

Sailing Away

I had always had a fascination for being on the water. It has played a huge part in my life in many ways. As well as all the friends I have made across the world in different fleets and the places I have been, the physical skills of boat handling and mental aspects of race tactics have subconscious subliminal effects on many aspects in life.

It started with those adventures with Huggins on the homemade raft off the beach at Silecroft and later at St. Annes with my friend and fellow apprentice at Rolls Royce, David Fleetwood. These had sown the seed.

In Foulridge, close to my then home at Lancashire Ghyll, are two feeder reservoirs for the Leeds and Liverpool Canal. They are, in fact, feeding the highest point of the canal where the mile tunnel, so called, cuts through the land on the route before heading off downhill once more. The country's east-west watershed runs through the village of Foulridge. Water spilt on one side of a certain wall in the village will end up in the Irish Sea whilst water spilt on the other side will head to the North Sea.

Burwain Sailing Club is situated on the lower reservoir and had not

Left: Burwain Sailing Club on the feeder reservoir for the Leeds & Liverpool Canal

Right: Susan Whittaker and I sailing a Firefly at Burwain. Susan was a lovely girl from Shadwell, Leeds, studying to be a doctor at Liverpool University. I was in love with her at the time

much more than a large hut for a clubhouse in the 1950s. I was 19 years old when I first went to the club with David Fleetwood. Being designers, we had the brilliant idea of designing and building our own sailing boat. It was to be a catamaran. They were fast and their modern looking designs were appealing.

We approached the Club Secretary, Walter Mitchell, with our ideas. He very diplomatically sank our initial plans. "Well, you do realise that, before you are allowed to bring this yacht to the club, you are going to have to test it for seaworthiness and prove that it is safe to sail?" He went on to persuade us that there was not much point in designing and building a new boat and perhaps it would be better to buy one of the existing dinghy classes at the club? These consisted of Burnham One Designs, Merlin Rockets, GP 14s and Firefly dinghies.

We decided on a Firefly and found one for sale at £120 (£2,700 today). We were earning £2 (£107.20 today) a week at the time as Rolls Royce apprentices so it took a good deal of saving up and financial juggling before we managed to buy our first boat, Firefly number 639, "Imshi". We did it by saving a pound a week.

On telling Uncle Phillip that I had bought a boat, he said, "You've bought a boat?" "Yes," I said. "Then you've only bought it to swank to your friends," was his conclusion – and I've been swanking ever since, it turns out.

A Firefly dinghy is twelve feet in length with 90 square feet of sail area having a jib and a mainsail. The hull construction is hot moulded

Left: My first Firefly, F639, "Imshi", on the home made road trailer made from the axle of an Austin 7, with the launching trolley upturned on top of the foredeck. Pictured here behind my parents' car at Lancashire Ghyll

ply using similar techniques to those employed in making the Mosquito twin engined fighter/bomber of the Second World War. The design came from Uffa Fox in 1946 and was an evolution of an earlier design of his. It was selected for the 1948 Olympics, held at Torquay, as the single-handed class but became popular as a two-man class soon afterwards. Significantly, the gold medal in the class at those Olympics was won by the famous Danish yachtsman, Paul Elvstrom, 18-years old at the time, who I was to meet much later in life.

We raced the boat on Sunday afternoons against the other Fireflies and gradually improved in performance. It took a while – it is not as easy as experienced sailors make it look. A Firefly can be quite tippy and we did find ourselves capsized more than once. I would often go home after sailing on a Sunday afternoon to be asked by brother Robert, "Have you been falling in again?"

We had adventures with the boat, too. I made a road trailer from the axle of an Austin Seven, with mast step and launching trolley. All was well engineered with technical calculations from lessons learnt at college. Perhaps I wasn't listening in class sufficiently or somehow made an error because the launching trolley collapsed. We young engineers were not yet perfect, it transpired. On analysis, we found an error in a moment of inertia figure – yes, we did go to such detail, we budding Brunels.

So we were mobile and Fleetwood, brother Robert and I towed the boat to Arnside, where we had our first excursion on the sea. It is not the best place to learn the ropes – the fierce tides and hidden sandbanks of the Kent estuary require respect. Timing was crucial so as not to be carried away by the strong currents down to Morecambe Bay

Below: A Firefly, with cotton sails and the Club's Starter's Box on the bank behind

or upstream and under the railway viaduct. But we had fun, survived and youth made light of the risks.

Later, I joined Club excursions to Abersoch in the summer where we would camp for a week or so. Burwain Sailing Club had, actually, been founded by members of South Caernarvonshire Yacht Club based at Abersoch. It extended the short sailing season for them as sailing at Burwain continued well into autumn instead of only to late August on the sea at Abersoch.

The Firefly was also ideal for team racing and this took place between rival clubs on a northern circuit from West Kirby to Royal Windermere and from Budworth to Hollingworth (where Brian Herron, a star Firefly sailor, thought my trailer was "…somewhat agricultural…").

I sailed at Burwain for many years – all through my time at Rolls Royce and Lucas Aerospace. Abersoch Dinghy Week, which was held each year by SCYC, signalled a mass exodus from Burwain to the seaside. Robin Delves, my old friend and fellow Firefly sailor at Burwain, would hire Cae Du Farm from 'Jones the Coal' who would migrate to his shed for the duration to make room. Robin and his family had the farmhouse and some of the Burwain sailors camped in tents and caravans in the field. I took the tent that mother had made and towed down the Firefly, as did several of the Burwain and other northern club members to make up a reasonably sized fleet for the week.

In 1964 brother Robert and I went all the way to Christchurch, in Hampshire (but now in Dorset), towing the boat behind my MG TD, for an open meeting. The tent came in handy again as, to save money, we camped in the New Forest for the week. We finished in second place. It was quite an achievement for us and I still have the stoneware mug that we won as a prize.

After a few years, Robin and Robert Sunderland, another Burwain member, bought a Dragon, "Stormalong" – a larger keelboat of classic racing lines, which they kept at Abersoch. Robin took the helm and Robert and I crewed. My post was foredeck man. On one occasion, I hoisted the spinnaker upside down but nobody noticed. Not wanting to look an idiot, I said nothing. Eventually, but not until the last run home, the error was noticed. I got the well-deserved roasting. I could only afford to pay for the upkeep of the Dragon – the running costs. Robin and Robert bought the boat as I did not have funds available to chip in.

I remember Robert selling the Dragon and, when asked by a potential purchaser if it leaked and if we had to pump out the boat at all, he said that the boat was sound and we never had to pump. An absolute lie – we were forever pumping out the hull.

An older friend at Burwain was Tony Clegg – a worldly-wise survivor

Above: Camping at Abersoch. L to r: Jane & Max Uttley, Self, Christine Delves with daughter, Susan

Below: Dragon sailing at Abersoch

of the war. I sometimes used to crew for Tony in his Firefly, at Burwain or on Lake Windermere. He had a caravan there with his wife Sylvia. Post-wartime restrictions had made overseas travel pretty difficult so holidaying in Britain was the option. Tony was also a member at SCYC and had a cruising yacht at Abersoch, which we used to sail together during Abersoch Keel Boat Week in August. "Sinbad of Abersoch" was a brand new, state of the art, 37-foot long yacht, designed by Alan Buchanan and built by R. Pryor of Burnham. She was registered in Liverpool in 1961. I also did an Irish Sea race with Tony in "Sinbad".

The Burwain Annual Dinner and Dance was, at that time, held at the Craiglands Hotel in Ilkley, Yorkshire. (Many of the key players in the club were from the wealthier families in the Yorkshire textile trade.) I was 26 years old by then and working at Lucas. During dinner Tony broached the subject of going on a long cruise in "Sinbad", which would take several months – possibly across the North Sea to the waters of Skagerrak and Kattegat in Scandinavia. He was making last minute arrangements and asked if I would like to join him in his adventure. Without thinking of consequences, I immediately said, "Yes!" and could think of nothing else for the rest of the evening.

I was so excited at the prospect of a sea voyage that I nearly drove my car off the road on the way home. Coming over 'the Moss' (a fairly high road crossing the Pennines) I span the MG TD and only just recovered short of leaving the carriageway and going cross country.

The next week, at work at Lucas, I had to let the Chief Engineer, Ron Jackson, know my intentions. I tried to work out how I could possibly retain my position at the company but still go to sea with Tony for several months. In a previous year, Ron had taken a leave of absence to go on an expedition and climb Mount Everest. I wondered if I could

Above: In harbour, Newlyn

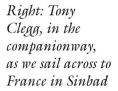

Right: Tony Clegg, in the companionway, as we sail across to France in Sinbad

play the same card. No chance. Ron, quite correctly, determined that my frolickings were not an 'expedition' but a holiday. So reluctantly I had to resign from Lucas Aerospace. My parents, understandably, were most upset. Mother had managed to take this dyslexic boy and somehow push, encourage, tutor and manoeuvre him into a career and position not thought remotely likely from the beginning. Now he was resigning a post well up the career ladder and it would not be easy to get back to that rung once off the ladder. They were livid.

The crew set off for Pwllheli harbour in North Wales where we were storm-bound for seven days. The weather was evil. We took the time to discuss plans and decided to amend our route and head for France and see if we could make it at all. Finally, the weather cleared and four of us set sail. We were Tony Clegg the owner/skipper, with Arthur Thompson – a manufacturer of shoes and a member of SCYC, John Riddle, another SCYC member, and myself.

We were not good at navigating to say the least. I remember having to get out my road atlas and point out where Lundy Island was in relation to where we were and our intended route to the Bristol Channel, Lands End and Newlyn, our destination. We finally arrived at Newlyn by some amazing stroke of luck – it was not judgement – and spent a night in port preparing for the next step in our adventure – the crossing of the English Channel to the Brittany coast of France.

Again, on this next leg, our navigational skill was lacking. The only tool we had was the Decca radio network receiver. This, theoretically,

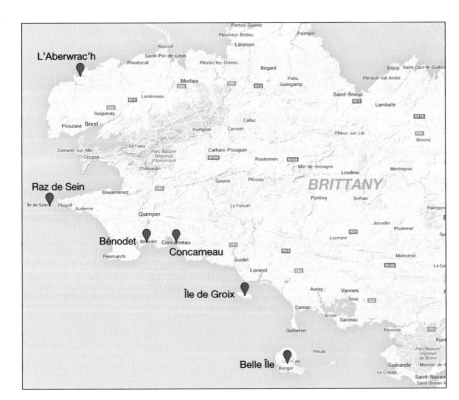

Left: The landmarks on the French adventure

Map image: © Google.com

allowed us to plot our position based on the pattern created by the interaction of several radio transmitters. As I said, theoretically. Theory was not put into practice at all successfully but the French fishermen we met off the French coast were very helpful in guiding us in the right direction. We reached L'Aberwrac'h in Brittany and planned our onward journey towards the south of France.

Tony and the team would return to England periodically leaving me in charge of the boat until their return. Alone one evening, I had gone ashore in the dinghy, tying it to a wooden jetty whilst I went into the village for food. I may have had a few drinks too many in the local café as when I returned to the jetty the tide had come in and covered it. I had tied the dinghy to the jetty with too short a rope. The dinghy had risen on the tide as far as possible before being retained at the bow by the painter, pulling the bow down toward the surface of the water where it was in danger of going under. In rather a panic I ran down towards the flooded jetty with the intention of reaching down into the water to try to find the painter and untie the boat. As I reached the jetty I heard shouting behind me and a Frenchman, who seemed extremely concerned for my safety, grabbed me. However hard I tried to explain that I was trying to rescue the dinghy, not knowing any French, I was not understood. No matter how I tried to escape and get down to the boat he would not let me go. His intense concern

Below: Sinbad under sail

39

Above: Part of the power plant of the Rover BRM at Le Mans? They certainly look like turbine blades

eventually led me to believe that he thought I was trying to take my own life. He wasn't going to let that happen at any cost. I spent a cold night on a bench.

My job was to make sure that the yacht was spick and span for the return of the crew. One job I had was to clean the teak decks with a lemon. There must be a reason for this but I never knew it. Tony was meticulous. Being 13 years my senior he became a mentor. He showed me how to check the rigging and replace any lengths that looked worn and many other safety issues that might need addressing. As the boat was winterised he made a detailed inventory of all the equipment removed so none was forgotten. He was extremely safety conscious. When he entered for the Fastnet race, for instance, he equipped the boat with brand new rigging throughout.

Tony, Sylvia and their friends would arrive for the next leg of the voyage. I was considered to be the cabin boy. I could not cook, though. I still cannot cook – at all. On the third attempt at presenting a breakfast of bacon and eggs to the guests one morning, it was thrown over the side and Tony had to take over. I think I was very nearly thrown over the side with the breakfast.

We travelled down the French coast as far as the Ile de Groix, sailing through the Raz de Sein to Bénodet and Concarneau. On one stopover I made a spur of the moment decision to go to Le Mans for the 24 hour race. I arrived there on the train and took a taxi. When we got to the track, the driver asked if I would like to drive around the circuit. I said "Yes" of course and he obliged.

He also tried to help me find accommodation, realising that I would struggle with my lack of the language. We failed to find anything. Had I thought about it for a moment before setting off I would have realised that would be the case on such a busy weekend. After tramping around trying to find a bed I eventually gave up and, in the dark,

Right: Pit-side at Le Mans

wandered into a nearby wood for some sort of shelter. I spent a night in my waterproofs in the open but was tired enough from the journey to fall asleep.

On rising in the morning, I shook off some stiffness and looked around to get my bearings. The track must be over there, I thought, so set off. When I reached the track I was amazed to discover that I was "pit-side". No one challenged me at all so I spent a fantastic day exploring the pits and team garages with great interest. Coincidentally, one car running that year was powered by the Rover-BRM gas turbine engine not totally dissimilar to the Rotax ones we worked on at Lucas.

Above: In the cockpit, I'm on the left, with the dinghy secured on the cabin roof

Our voyage in Sinbad lasted three months in all. I learnt a lot in that time from the variety of friends that turned up as crew. They were all from Tony's time in life and most had served in the war. Tony had been a Major in the Indian Army. The war was a frequent topic of conversation with Tony enquiring if his friends had "…had a good war?" Many a tale of war experiences, life and love were recounted. The 'man talk' could be explicit: some of the sexual recountings were

Left: Sinbad in one of the French ports. Note the French courtesy flag at the crosstrees

most startling to me at the time. I think I must have led a relatively sheltered life up until then.

One Saturday in February 2010, Gilles Graham invited me to go and see his new yacht. He was sailing with an old friend of mine, Adam Gosling, whose father is Sir Donald Gosling who owns a fantastic super yacht, Leander.

They duly arrived, as arranged, at 1 p.m., picking up a mooring just off the pontoon at Fiddlers where the yacht was going to be permanently based. We were ferried out to her and, as I stepped on to the boat, I had the feeling I might have seen her before. I was told that she was an Alan Buchanan design built by R. Pryor at Burnham in 1961. I had not only seen her before, I'd sailed on her down to the coast of France all those years ago. When I looked at the mainsheet traveller I could vividly remember making the little stainless steel paddle screws to stop the mainsheet sliding about in the track.

The fact that I can now look out from my house on the Beaulieu River across the water to where Sinbad is moored is such a remarkable coincidence that it suggests to me a higher power.

Tony Clegg played such an important part in my life. Whilst on our tremendous trip, he travelled frequently to and from England on business. He was a very successful businessman. On one of his trips he bought a small engineering company, Drum Pumps in Bradford. I had never heard of it: I was about to.

Right: Sinbad of Cowes, as she has been renamed, moored in the Beaulieu River, 2015

Chapter 5

Back to Reality

I was offered a job as soon as we got back to England. It was not going to help my career. Back in Abersoch, we visited the Porth Tocyn Hotel – an upmarket establishment high on the hill with splendid views of the bay and the town. The owner, Mr. Fletcher Brewer, said, "We think you are a very fine young man and we can offer you a job behind the bar or waiting on tables." I declined the offer. Mr. Brewer would never know how lucky he was that he avoided my lack of talent in those areas.

As it happened, Tony Clegg had offered me the chance to apply for a position at his recent company acquisition, Drum Engineering. He was looking for someone to take on the post of Assistant Chief Engineer. The post did not look very inviting initially as the salary on offer was only £1,000 per annum (about £18,000 today) compared with my previous salary at Lucas of £1,300 (about £25,000 today) – a significant drop.

On my first visit to Drum I was dismayed. The buildings and the shop floor were so old fashioned and a stark contrast to the high level of technology and order at Rolls or Lucas. The power to the production machines was transmitted by the old overhead shaft and belts system inherited from the textile mills. It was like stepping back in time and looked as though it could be a backward step for me too.

I had grown close to Tony and trusted him. The carrot he dangled in front of me now was sufficient temptation to draw me in. As the current Chief Engineer was getting on in years, the new Assistant Chief would be expected to take on the role on his retirement at the much more attractive salary level of over £2,250 (about £42,500 today) per annum.

I decided to apply – I had no alternative positions in mind or on offer. Collecting together the reports, calculations, designs, reference books and drawings for projects undertaken when working at Rolls and Lucas, I drove back to Bradford for an interview.

My previous work was at a much higher technical level than anything produced at Drum. The calculations for jet engine turbine blades and other projects must have left them rather dumbfounded. They did actually say that I was "...much too good for us." They offered me the job in any case and I accepted.

The huge difference between Drum and my previous employers

was the scale of operation – the sheer size and numbers being so much smaller than I was used to. This smaller size meant that one made contact with much more of the overall production and commercial functions of a company's operations. People had to overlap into adjacent aspects of a project. It was the first time that I had come across a Sales Department and the requirements of selling a product. I gained an awful lot of experience in the wider world of running a business. It was at Drum that I was introduced to the road transport industry and its market for products associated with the transportation of liquids. This was another key moment in my history and was to open the gates to the source of my future commercial success. Drum produced pumps, valves and other equipment for liquid handling as part of their production.

The smaller size of company also meant that there was far less inertia and decisions were made more quickly: designs were agreed, detailed and put into production in weeks rather than years. I could design a new product – or modify an existing one – then take it to the customer to explain its merits and obtain the order. I would travel down to London to visit customers such as Shell with new ideas.

We had an agent in Malaysia who sold pumps for palm oil as one line of business. The directors at Drum put in a request for a small pump of similar functionality but for use specifically with fuel oil – and I developed this concept into a detailed design. I was called to the Board meeting in front of the Directors to submit my design and drawings – something I had not experienced previously and which was a little daunting at first.

I presented my design for the small pump – which we had christened the 'Husky'. The Directors studied the drawings, discussed the merits of the design and announced that they approved and that "… we will authorise 100 of these to be manufactured immediately." I was dumbfounded – and elated. This was the very first time a product designed and detailed by me was to go into commercial production: a veritable landmark for me personally.

At Lucas and Rolls Royce we never had the opportunity to put forward our own ideas and designs, never mind get them into production. The Board at Drum, on the other hand, could quickly recognise potential in a new design and approve it for production without the inertia of bureaucracy.

My time at Drum was a period of intense, committed working in an environment where I learnt an awful lot. But it was interesting and absorbing work: it was full of detail and action. Design problems such as the failure of a particular pump were challenging and intricate in their analysis. The pump problem was isolated to an issue with the bearings and the solution involved meetings with the bearing manufacturers and the use of special Hoffman bearings. These replaced the inappropriate original bearings and solved the problem of the pumps failing. The solution sounds simple but it was the identification of the problem that was making the pumps fail that took the effort. It was to save the product and a considerable amount of money for the Company.

I may be accused of being rather full of myself shortly afterwards. I designed a four-way valve. It was an excellent product – an efficient design. I was very pleased with the work I had done in producing the design and drawings. The valve controlled the flow of product in two directions, which allowed pumps to pump liquids out, as in discharging, or suck liquid in, as in loading road tankers. I gave it

Left: Sales literature for the Drum 3-way valve, which was redesigned by me as the 4-way valve

45

a name – the "Fort Four-way Valve". The Sales Director quickly knocked me back into place and it was named the "Drum Four-way Valve" – quite rightly. Bill Ruffle did not want to give the upstart Fort any higher standing in the company than he deserved.

I knew I was being cocky but perhaps I was beginning to realise that I could design practical and commercially viable products myself – independently and even under my own brand name.

Chapter 6

A Shocking Surprise Purchase

As we walked onto the shop floor of the modern factory an eerie sight met us. Hundreds and hundreds of old machine tools were ranked in untidy rows as far as the eye could see. What made the sight so eerie was the silence, the inactivity, not normally met in such a place.

It was September, 1966 and my life generally was very pleasant at that period of time. At the age of 29 I was comfortably living at home with my parents – a great benefit when it comes to housekeeping, having meals prepared and providing a warm and secure base. I had a car, a good circle of friends at the sailing club, close to home in Foulridge, and my own boat that I enjoyed racing.

My job at Drum Engineering in Bradford was good. I was very happy there, working in the Design Office as Assistant Chief Engineer under Dudley Marshall. Dudley was due to retire in the not-too-distant future and the promise of my stepping into his shoes as Chief Engineer encouraged me to continue with the company.

The shop floor at Drum, although old-fashioned in a lot of ways, was always busy, noisy and full of life – which is what, in contrast, gave the rows of dead production machines we gazed upon in this barren, silent shop floor such a strange and unnatural atmosphere. Wires hung loose, not connected; dust and dirt abounded; oil leaked onto the floor; machines lay at awkward angles; cabinets stood balanced on top of machines instead of neatly alongside. It was all rather disturbing to a mind used to precision and order.

I was there with John Marsh, Production Engineer at Drum. We had seen an advertisement in the Yorkshire Post inserted by the Ministry of Defence (MoD), Directorate of Sales. The MoD was selling production machine tools that were now surplus to requirements. They were machines originally engaged in war production – some from the Second World War and some producing for the Korean War (1950 – 53) which had ended only 13 years before. The machines had been collected from shadow factories up and down the country and put on display in this modern building near Yeadon, close to Leeds/Bradford Airport, for viewing prior to sale by sealed bid.

As we walked through the ranks of dead machines, I had to rely on John to explain what the machines that caught our eye were designed to do. There were various types of machine tools – capstan lathes, lathes, very special jig boring machines and a whole host of machine tools needed to make armaments for the navy, air force and the army. The machines were for producing the ordnance required for the full armed forces. I didn't have much of a clue about the more specialised machines such as jig borers or surface grinders and relied on John's expertise when trying to assess which machines still had some usable life in them. Although old, many of the machines on view would be capable of efficient work with a little TLC, John explained.

"So people could think that some of these machines might be worth buying?" I asked.

"Oh yes," John said, "Some of these machines will carry on working for donkeys' years. They were solidly made – made to last."

There were several people walking around with us, some in groups, some singly. Many were jotting information into notebooks and were studying particular machines of interest. They prodded and poked; looked under and around; lifted covers and inspected innards; then wrote some more. Most were studying the more general machines – the lathes and pedestal drills – machines that would sell on easily in the trade. "Those guys will be machine dealers," John explained, "looking to buy cheap and sell on quickly. They won't be interested in the very specialized machines."

We continued our stroll around the factory, stopping occasionally at a particular machine that caught John's eye. He would inspect more closely the details of the working parts – the chuck, the beds, whatever (I didn't really know what he was inspecting or why). Watching him, listening to his comments, I got the feeling there was some 'worth' to these old beasts, that there might be life in the old dogs yet. The little grey cells were stirring.

"So what might this machine be worth?" I asked.

"Something like this? – perhaps a 1950 machine – good maker – good size – it might go for something around £2,500," said John, the equivalent of £42,000 in 2016. We walked along many and various rows. The machines weren't laid out in groups of type so we would come across machines of interest by chance and John would give me a résumé of their function, performance and likely value. But it was all getting a little too detailed for me. I barely understood more than the basics of what he explained. My capacity for absorbing information had been reached. I did, however, remember the values.

When we had arrived at the viewing, we each were given a tender form. I'd popped it in a pocket, not thinking of ever using it. Casually putting hands in pockets as we walked, I felt the piece of paper, pulled it out and scanned over the format.

"Shall we have a punt?" I laughingly asked John. "Why don't we put in an offer for a couple of machines? You never know, we might bag a bargain!" John was used to my larking around but picked out a few machines and indicated what they might be worth.

I jotted down on the offer form derisory figures – Lot 5: £285 (£4,790 today) – instead of the £2,400 (about £40,000 today) – for a Precimax Fine Boring Machine: Lot 36: £265 (£4,500 today) for a Keighley Plunge Grinder, worth around the same as the Precimax, according to John. Altogether I put in bids for ten individual machines. If a guide price was there, I would put in an offer of around ten percent. It was purely as a joke with absolutely no intention of making a purchase at all.

We both laughed and the tender form went back into the pocket and it stayed there. So, having been suitably entertained for the afternoon, we went home.

Work at Drum continued to be enjoyable as I became more involved in the wider range of commercial activities that a small company with limited staff has to practice. One star employee was my secretary, a young lady called Kathleen Bedford. She was a person who had to deal with all kinds of administrative issues for everyone and every department as well as for me. Her wide-ranging brief made her extremely knowledgeable in all aspects of the company operations. She was most helpful to me personally and we got on extremely well, at work and socially.

It was Kathleen who, some days following my visit to Yeadon, reminded me about the tender form which was still in my pocket. I'd told her about the machines and how we'd jokingly jotted down some silly offer prices but not submitted the form. Having a bit more commercial experience, Kathleen knew that sometimes really low

Left: Kathleen Bedford, we were out on a weekend walk together in the Dales

offers for machinery can get accepted – she'd seen it happen before. I didn't believe it. Who would let a machine go for a couple of hundred pounds when it was worth over £2,000?

"You have seen the date on the form by which offers have to be received, haven't you?" Kathleen asked. "I think you should get that form in the post today."

I was persuaded to post the form – to have a joke more than anything. The post was going at 4 o'clock in the afternoon and that day was the last chance to get the form in the post if the offer was to reach the MoD in time. We did it. I signed the form and Kathleen got it in the post. We had a laugh and a joke telling John Marsh what we'd done – and thought no more about it.

A month passed by. Then, on returning home after work one day,

Right: The original invoice for the two machines bought as the shocking result of my joke offer

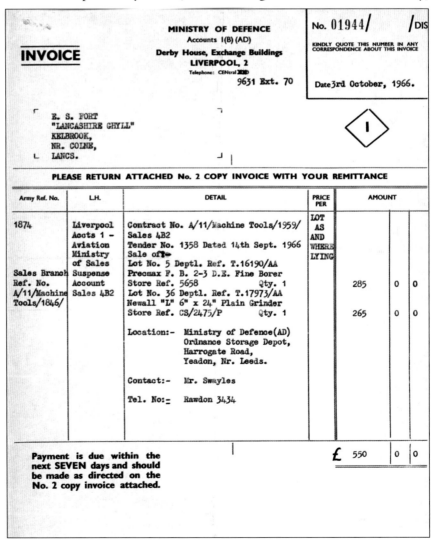

my mother said that I'd received a letter – it was in a "very peculiar yellow envelope" and from the MoD.

The penny didn't drop. The envelope was indeed an unusual colour – not the usual buff or white. It was from the MoD. It didn't ring any bells. I opened the envelope and nearly died! My offer for two of the machines had been accepted! Lot 5 and lot 36. I owed the Directorate of Sales £550.00 (£9,240 today). What a bombshell.

I had to sit down, collapsing almost – mind racing, heart beating hard and fast – and read the note again. "This acceptance creates a contract…." "…no payment should be made until you receive… an invoice… due within 7 days…" "… date from which you will have 28 days to remove the machines…"

What had I done? This was supposed to be a bit of a joke – it was not serious but now, suddenly, it was. My larking about had got me into real trouble. Mother realized something shattering had happened.

"What's wrong, lad?" she said.

I was, in my mind, rapidly working through some alternative courses of action – ways forward, out of this mess. My heartbeat steadied a little but my thoughts were still racing. Could I claim to have made a mistake? Could I go to the directors at Drum and say that I'd bought the machines on behalf of the company? Where was I going to put them? What on earth were they? What did they do? Where was I to get the money on my meagre salary?

Mother read the note and I could tell by the way she picked up the edge of her apron and wiped her hands with it that she was shocked and worried. But she said nothing and let me think.

I had no idea what to do. A sleepless night lay ahead. My stomach just would not stop churning. My thoughts were racing, colliding, not getting anywhere. Whatever happened now, this was the biggest, most alarming and sickening point in my life to date.

Chapter 7

Going it Alone

After recovering from the shell-shock of receiving the invoice from the Ministry of Defence for the two machines bought on the back of a joke, I began to apply some much-needed logic to the situation.

Firstly, I had to find out just what I had bought. I was not sure of the size of the machines; how heavy they were; what they did. I raced over to the factory in Yeadon to find out and discovered that I had quite a logistical problem. Also, I would need a substantial workshop: commercial engineering premises. These machines were not going to fit in at my parents' farm barn. I had not ever considered that my derisory offers for the machines might be accepted. The thought that I might actually end up owning them never entered my head.

Up to this point, I had absolutely no intention of running my own business. That was never the plan. The purchase of the two machines forced my hand. Without any other viable course of action, it seemed inevitable that I would have to establish and run an engineering business of my own. I had already begun to realise that I was capable of designing a product and getting it to market. I thought I had enough experience of commercial activities and I was being encouraged by my lovely, supportive Kathleen.

I went over the problems with Father at home, and we started a hunt for premises. Businesses were thriving at the time, however, and there were not many suitable premises available. We both kept looking as time allowed. We only had 21 days to remove the machines from the Yeadon mill.

I left Drum Engineering in December 1966. Word had got around that I was starting an engineering business and a customer of Drum's contacted me on the very day I was leaving. It was George Lambert of Kenning Road Tankers, based in Ossett, Yorkshire. He rang and said he had a project that I might be able to work on.

On visiting his office, he showed me an existing valve produced by Audco. The challenge was to reduce the weight of the valve by half. Weight is an important factor in the production of road tankers and every little helps. I listened, examined the valve and said that I thought I could achieve the desired result with an improved design.

Back home at Lancashire Ghyll, I started work on the project in my workshop. I developed the basic design, produced all the assembly and component drawings and technical specifications. I also created

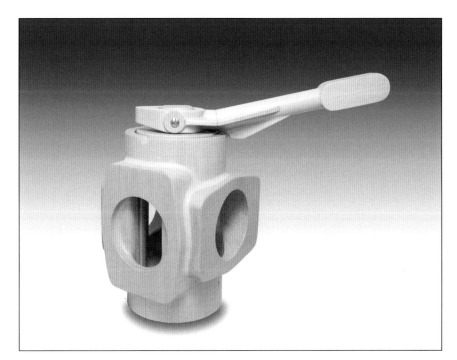

a wooden model with moving parts to illustrate the function and prove the mechanical action. There followed a detailed and impressive quotation document and an accompanying technical manual.

On the basis of these, George Lambert gave me an order for one hundred units – with the proviso that an initial batch of five prototype valves functioned well and reliably. As ever, Uncle Phillip had advice, albeit negative, "You can't be going into valves, lad, it's a very competitive industry."

In the meantime Father had heard from his partner in business, Harry Carey, that a workshop might be available on Norfolk Street in Colne. Stephen Pickles, who, coincidentally, lived behind Burwain Sailing Club, had got into financial difficulties. He needed to raise some money and was selling the Norfolk Street premises for £2,500 (over £42,000 today). They were perfect for my needs but I did not have that sort of money available for the purchase – it was an awful lot of money in those days. What could have been a dream start looked at the time as though it would slip away and a golden chance would escape. I was going to do my damndest to capitalise on the opportunity and approached Father for support. We met Pickles at the premises on Norfolk Street. To my wonderful relief my father offered straight away to buy the premises; "If you want the premises lad, I'll buy them for you". At last I would have somewhere to install the two machines. My first premises were bought in 1966 and the business began in 1967.

The two machines I had bought were not at all suitable equipment for starting an engineering business. They were very specialised in their function and top quality, very expensive machines when new. I had absolutely no experience of using these machines or their operation. I thought I may have made a terrible mistake but, as it turned out, by another amazing coincidence these two very specialist machines would prove perfect and crucial to the manufacture of this new valve for which I had the order. I could hardly believe this stroke of luck.

This first-ever Fort Vale Engineering product was a 2 ½" cast iron, 'T'-port, three-way valve. The Precimax SMX FV23 fine boring machine was absolutely fundamental to achieving the accuracy of the three-inch diameter bore. The L12 Keighley Plunge Grinder was also key in the grinding of the valve plug. Without these two specific machines it would have been totally impossible to manufacture the valve.

This series of coincidental yet pivotal key moments was set to follow me through life and tease me forever with the concept of a higher power controlling my destiny.

Both of these very specialist machines were also actually manufactured locally as well. The Plunge Grinder was made in Keighley – the clue's in the name. It had a grinding wheel three inches wide with a diameter of over two feet – a most capable machine indeed. The Precimax was made in Cowling, not far from Colne. We visited the factory, much later, and were given red-carpet treatment when we asked about some extra tooling for the machine to perform a particular operation. When I received the quotation for the work to be done, I realised just why we had been treated so well. The price was astronomical and brought

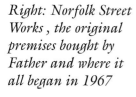

Right: Norfolk Street Works , the original premises bought by Father and where it all began in 1967

home to me just how high was the quality of the machine I had bought so cheaply. A new machine was many thousands of pounds. We did not buy the extra tooling from the manufacturers but made it ourselves.

One day, when Father was in the works, he managed to push the wrong button on the grinder and sent the wheel on a fast traverse directly into the dressing diamond, smashing it to pieces. (After using the grinder, the grinding wheel was 'dressed' or given a true grinding surface again using an industrial diamond tool to 'clean' the surface.) I was livid but could not be angry with Father who was always so supportive. It was just one of those things but it puzzled the accountants when the purchase of a nine carat diamond appeared on the paperwork.

"What on earth does an engineer want with a nine carat diamond?" asked Derek Evans, no doubt suspecting some devious transaction. It was explained to him.

Although these two machines would be perfect for one element of the first production runs, more machines were needed for other operations necessary to complete the manufacture of the valves. I needed a lathe and various other bits and pieces – pillar drills, grinding wheels, etc., as well as having to kit out the small office and even smaller drawing office. This all needed further finance. I had the bare shell of a building and was starting from scratch. Here I was, employee number one of Fort Vale Engineering and the only employee for the moment.

With the building secured I was able to invite the bank manager of the Midland Bank for a meeting – held over dinner at my parents'

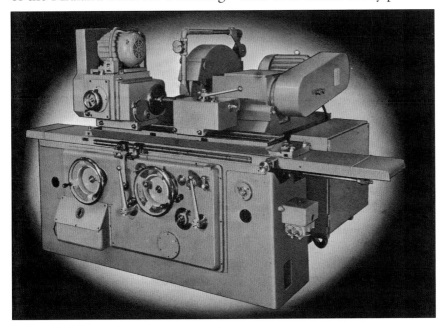

Left: The L12 Keighley Plunge Grinder, which was fundamental in the production of the first Fort Vale valves

Above: Robert Fort, my younger brother and Fort Vale employee No. 2

farmhouse. With the outline of the business discussed and with the benefit of current orders, I was granted an overdraft facility of £5,000 (about £84,000 today) and was able to move forward. This was only agreed, however, on the condition that the deeds to the Norfolk Street premises were lodged at the bank. The property was not mine, of course, but Father's. I am happy to say that family support remained firm and the deeds were so lodged. You may ask how I managed to set up and run a business on so little capital, even in those days. The answer is – with hard work and ensuring that every penny counted.

All this time, with so much going on, I was still working one day a week consultancy at Drum and half a day design work at Waddington of Leeds, the manufacturer of board games, which I knew through Berwick Watson, son of the managing director there.

Another key move at this time was to persuade younger brother Robert to join me in the company. I had been working alone for one month. Robert was working at the BBC in London at the time. He was involved with lighting and the technical side of sets. He had always been interested in the theatre and had taken jobs for various local theatre companies (living in terrible digs, much to Mother's consternation) on the technical side after leaving university. There, he had won an award for the production of the play, "Serjeant Musgrave's Dance" but his commitment to the theatre had robbed him of time and he never passed his examinations.

Robert was Fort Vale employee number 2, helping me from the very beginning. I always referred to him as my 'secret weapon' on the shop floor. He was incredibly talented at quickly identifying the key qualities of a machine and using them to best advantage in production. He shunned limelight in the company: hated going to award ceremonies: and was very supportive of the church in Kelbrook, where he now lies next to my parents. We worked together for his entire life and he died, tragically, at the young age of 62 years. In his honour, an apprenticeship achievement award has been established at Fort Vale Engineering.

It was together with Robert that the specification for a new lathe was drawn up. In typical fashion, Robert had worked out what operations we needed to perform in production and determined the size of lathe we needed. Top of the range lathe company at the time was Dean, Smith and Grace but they were way too expensive for our budget. We travelled to Harrison Lathes in Cleckheaton in our tired-looking old motor car and arrived at the gatehouse to the factory, to be quizzed by the security man. He was most surprised when we claimed to be there to buy a lathe. We obviously looked nothing like potential purchasers.

We had determined that what we needed was a thirteen-inch swing lathe and after walking around the shop floor with the sales team there,

I placed the order. As an afterthought, I turned to one of the fitters working on one of the machines. I asked his opinion on what might make the best investment for the sort of production engineering we were undertaking. His advice was to have nothing to do with the small lathe we had chosen but to go for the much larger seventeen-inch machine. I took his advice and changed the order. This larger machine was twice the price of the smaller. It was a huge decision, certainly the biggest financial decision I had taken to date. At the age of 30 years I decided to put my entire savings of £2,495 (nearly £42,000 today) into the purchase of the seventeen-inch Harrison. The lathe proved to be a great success, a worthy purchase, and became the backstay of our valve production over many years. Since then, I quite often talk to machine operators and value their opinion highly, as it is based on hands-on experience.

We had a very busy three months up to the point where we could start production in March 1967. All the machines had to be positioned, wired up and commissioned ready to start work.

Frank Hall and I installed all the initial electrical wiring at Norfolk Street for the first machines and for the machines that followed. Frank was a friend from Colne and one of the crowd of Huggins, Jack Smart, James Ilott and his brother John. James went on to be the last ever

Below: The production drawings were all done by me. This is a drawing for the machining of the cast iron body of the T-port valve

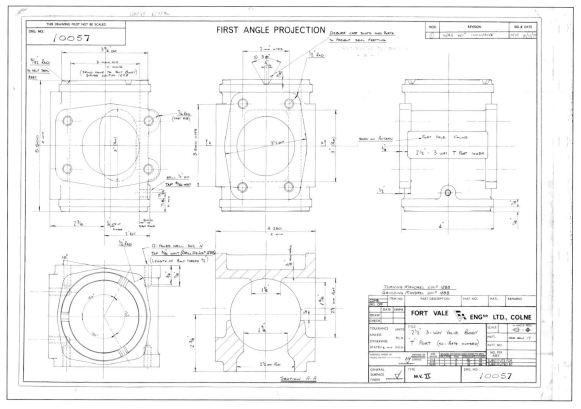

*Right: Living
at home with my
supportive parents
was a huge help*

mayor of Colne in 1973. We would meet after church and, when older, often end up in the pub together, or even in several pubs.

Frank was an electrician and has played such an important role in the development of Fort Vale over many decades. We worked in the evenings and at weekends as Frank was still working full time for Websters, the electricians in Burnley. He did all this as a pal, unpaid, and I acted as electrician's mate for the installation of those early machines – and not a very good one. I well remember him criticising my work – I was not deburring the metal edges of the trunking sufficiently. I was a very poor electrical apprentice, so that was never going to be a career option for me, obviously.

Frank reminds me that he never got any money for this work but that he has "… a drawer full of thank you letters." In my defence, he's been gainfully employed with plenty of work since.

The office administration had to be organised too. Kathleen Bedford helped tremendously in organising that part of the company and making sure that the paperwork ran smoothly. We had to be very careful of course as she was still working full-time at Drum and I, too, one day a week. It was particularly sensitive as the first production orders were coming to Fort Vale via Drum.

Mother and Father were always very supportive as well. Having a good home base with three good meals a day and no worries about domestic affairs made all the difference. With Robert there now too, it was a complete family effort.

The prototypes had worked well in the field and the complete order for the full batch of 100 'T'-port valves had come in. I had committed myself to the purchase of the castings and the jigs and fixtures prior to this, being so confident of the design. It had been a risk but made the manufacture of the prototypes much more efficient. Mind you, had the order been cancelled, it would have been a heavy loss to accommodate. The decision had proved to be a good one, thankfully. The valve continued to be successful and reliable in the field and became a leading product fitted to all the fuel oil delivery vehicles in the UK.

Above: The cover to the chute for sliding steel bar deliveries down to the cellar following the 'Colditz Shift'

Orders continued to flow in and Fort Vale supplied some 1,500 valves per year of this type alone. We were able to obtain twice the hourly rate for our machining work by selling our own product than we would have achieved as sub-contract engineers. Another key factor was that the product was very specific or 'niche' – a factor that has been consistently important in our range of equipment produced and marketed over the years.

We soon ran out of space in our Norfolk Street premises, which were only 2,500 square feet in area. Premises locally were still in short supply in 1967/68. Our solution was to dig for victory. The idea called the 'Colditz Shift'. At 6 p.m. each evening, after a full days work, we would start to dig out underneath the premises, extending the small basement underneath the footpath in front of the building. We engaged two labourers from the Town Council workforce in Colne to help us. After about a month we had extended the area and moved the building's foundations sufficiently to install a chute from the pavement above down into the basement so that steel supplies – long lengths of bar stock, etc., – could be delivered directly into our newly formed sawing section in the basement. The chute was topped with a steel plate hatch cover, which can still be seen in the pavement today.

The new space created also housed a valve assembly and testing area. This solution to a problem typified our approach at the time – we found a way around it and usually succeeded with a bit of thought and hard graft.

Kathleen continued to keep the administration efficient – making sure that quotations and letters were neat and professional and that all the other very necessary office functions ran smoothly. She was still working at Drum full time and continuing the subterfuge. I was still there too, for one day a week until the inevitable happened.

Tony Clegg called me into his office and he was not smiling. He could no longer ignore the fact that some of the work I was doing there was benefiting my own company. "Are you working on designs for a compressor?" he demanded. I had to admit it. "But we make compressors here – you don't!" he remonstrated. He did not hesitate for long. It was that time – time to part company.

With a sigh he said, "You're sacked." And that was that.

I was still able, through Kathleen, to keep an ear to the ground and

*Right: Kathleen
Bedford on the
beach at Abersoch*

learn what was happening at Drum. We continued to see each other
and developed a very close relationship. As well as seeing each other
in the office, we would meet at weekends and have various trips out
– whether walking in the Dales or sailing at Arnside or Abersoch with
brother Robert and his wife, Joanna.

It finished abruptly and unexpectedly. I called at her house in
Bradford one Saturday afternoon as I usually did but when Kathleen
opened the door, she kept me on the doorstep. "I'm afraid, Ted Fort",
she said, "my work for you has finished. I don't want to see you any
more." I simply burst into tears there and then. She had meant so
much to me and had been so supportive, much like my mother if I
think about it. It was all very sad.

Kathleen died of cancer at the age of 47, much too young, and it
wasn't until her death that I learnt of her age. I was surprised to find
out that she was nine years older than me. It had never occurred to
me that this might be the case. I wonder if she already knew or, at
least, had some inkling of her medical issues when she dismissed me
so suddenly. Or was it that she had been put under some pressure at
Drum to break the relationship? There was certainly some intelligence
gathering underway for my benefit and I wondered if the closeness
of our relationship had been discovered, despite our discretion, and
had been judged as unacceptable by the management at Drum. It was
never clarified for me.

As in any start-up business, money was very tight and we were
running at a loss initially. For the first nine months we were losing
money. Yet bills and wages needed to be paid; extra machines had to be

purchased to keep production flowing and efficient. Our accountants at the time were concerned. They were Hargreaves, Brown and Benson in Colne, with whom we have continued to be associated for many years now. I was asked by Derek Evans, Chief Accountant there at the time, whether I had any qualifications for getting another job for if we went bankrupt.

When I approached our bank, the Midland Bank in Colne, for an increase in our overdraft facility to £10,000 (over £160,000 today), the manager there said, "Are you looking at me through rose tinted spectacles this morning, Mr. Fort?" I was declined.

Derek Evans, however, introduced me to another Colne bank and the manager there, Cledwyn Thomas. His bank was eventually acquired and became the National Westminster Bank. Cledwyn was very astute and I like to think he was a good reader of character and business acumen. Whether it was this or the fact that Derek introduced me I am unaware, but I was granted the increased overdraft. I have since learnt, through his assistant at the time (and sailor), David Pratt, that Cledwyn had taken quite a risk in granting the level of overdraft facility so highly on the business evidence supplied. He trusted me enough to go out on a limb for me where no other bank would. We have continued to bank with that very same branch ever since and have channelled many millions of pounds through their doors.

After Cledwyn retired, I asked him to become my Financial Secretary and he faithfully performed that duty until he became too ill to continue.

We soon turned the corner to profitability. I had once worked out some performance figures for a visit to the Department of Trade and Industry in Manchester. I like to relate figures to a real life metaphor by way of illustration. Our thirteen workers at the time, I calculated, were turning out the equivalent of thirteen Mini cars a month. This related to a turnover of around £8,000 (around £131,000 today) with the price of a Mini being about £600 then. The comment from the staff at the DTI was "What size of whips do you use at your works?" The more impressive figure was the profit (gross) of £4,000 (about £65,000 today) on this turnover. This ratio of one mini per man per month still holds true, in round figures, in 2016.

We had been joined by Stuart Lowley to help on the sales side of the business. Stuart was experienced but expensive. We could only afford his services for a couple of days a week but he made all the difference. One thing we did together was to really explore the market. Leading on from our first product, the 'T'-port valve, we made an 'L'-port valve and looked at other products we could make for the same market – fuel oil delivery to central heating fuel tanks by AD Tankers (AD stands for 'Authorised Distributor'). Other products included

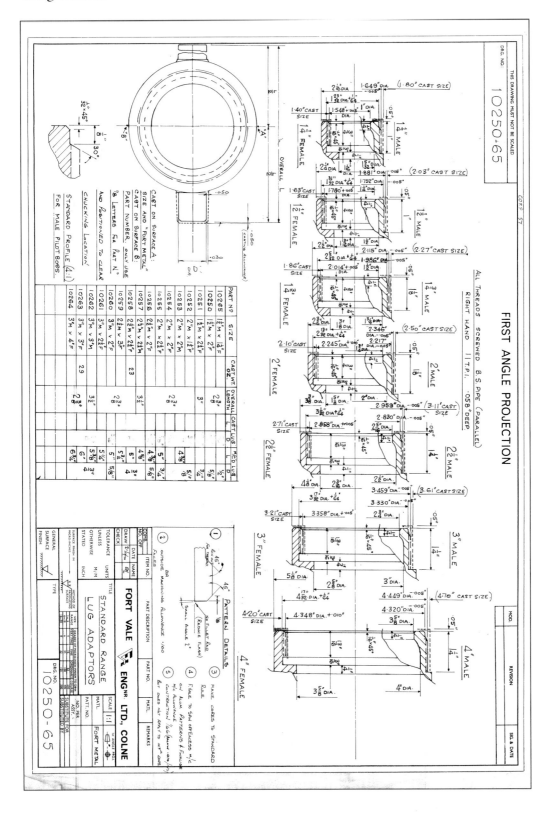

Left: The first Dufil lathe installed at Norfolk Street. I must have been working hard on the shop floor that day, looking at the state of my white coat. Rate of production using this machine on Fortmetal caps and adapters increased five-fold

hose reels, switch boxes, dipstick holders, couplings, power take-off flanges, adapters and caps for hoses. The most successful of these was the ball valve delivery nozzle which competed with the Scully version very successfully and became an industry standard. One thing that sticks in my mind about this early product in particular is the very expensive quick release threading taps required in the manufacture. OK – that's a detail too far but it does demonstrate the level at which my mind was working – and still does.

During our investigation of the market, Stuart and I had cause to visit Haddon Metals, a company in Hampshire selling aluminium alloy fittings, the metal composition of which had unusual characteristics. It was an alloy developed by the Germans in the Second World War we were told, to give the same durability and strength as gunmetal with much cheaper component metals. Our industry used many adapters, caps and other fittings in either aluminium, which had low wear and strength properties, or gunmetal, which was much more expensive. The owner of the company, Bill Williams, let us know from where he was getting his castings. We contacted the supplying company and managed to learn from them the composition of the alloy. It was then a simple matter to pass on this information to our own local casting company who supplied us with castings in this new alloy.

It was Stuart Lowley, with his marketing experience, who had the brilliant idea of calling the new material 'Fortmetal'. We started to make a wide range of fittings for the tank transport industry in Fortmetal at prices much lower than the gunmetal equivalent but still maintaining a huge profit margin for ourselves.

Opposite: Part of the range of adapters made from 'Fortmetal' – including the 10259. This is my original, extremely accurate and detailed production drawing

I was then introduced to an Italian firm that manufactured a profiling lathe called the Dufil. This machine was so efficient at machining caps and adapters from our new Fortmetal alloy that it increased production five-fold. Turning out these adapters at this phenomenal pace compared to the expensive gunmetal products was almost like printing money, it was so profitable. Fortmetal became a major wealth generator for the company and increased our market share enormously.

It was at this point that another uncanny coincidence revealed itself – this time in the form of numbers – that has followed me throughout my life. One of the Fortmetal adapters that was produced in the largest numbers was the 2½" male to 3" female BSP threaded adapter. Its part number was 10259.

259 – this number has occurred in my life so many times and with key associations or in life-changing coincidences. Sometimes it is all three figures, sometimes just the 59. It reinforces that niggling feeling I have that there may be a guiding hand playing out life for us all. It's there again and again. Or is it? Is it simply coincidence? I never fully convince myself that it can be purely coincidence: not with so much relevance and influence each time it occurs.

For a time, I was frightened that a competitor might also invest in a Dufil and ruin the advantage we had with our profitable line of products. I was also worried that I may not be fit enough to work the machine myself so I went off to the doctor for a check-up.

"What?" he exclaimed, "At your age? You're only 35 and you want a check-up?" He was flabbergasted. I explained about the new expensive

Right: A very young Frank Hall with David Huggins in David's converted London taxi. David's father would not have it on the drive looking like a taxi so David and Frank modified the bodywork! It still ran and took them both to Edinburgh on a proving trip

machine and that I had to be sure I'd be fit enough to operate it. It was difficult for the doctor to understand but it was simply that I wanted to make sure nothing would interrupt production by going wrong – not even my own health. I still have a medical check-up regularly and recommend that everyone does, once a year.

The pressure and pace at the time must have been quite a strain because Stuart Lowley resigned, saying, "I'd rather be a tame lion alive than an angry one dead."

We were up to that thirteen Mini mark with thirteen men in a well-balanced team. Key personnel were my brother, Robert and my old friend, Frank Hall, keeping the machines going whenever they broke down. We would call Frank out at any time of night to get the machines ready for the next day.

For many years, Frank was courting a very attractive young lady called Joyce. I was very attracted to Joyce myself and it got to the stage where I had to push Frank along a bit. "Look, Frank," I said one day, "you've been going out with Joyce for ages. It's getting to the point where you have to marry the girl – or I will!" He did and I didn't.

Father too helped in all sorts of supportive tasks. He would bring swing bolt forgings from the forge in tin boxes in the back of his Landrover and carry them, still hot, down the outside steps to the basement for machining. Taking drawings to the pattern makers for castings or fetching the castings when ready: these and many other jobs were very helpful. I believe he enjoyed these tasks in his retirement. Mother continued to look after us all. The family was still very much a part of things.

Other early workers included lathe operators Mick Meehan and Tom Preston who remained with the company until retirement. Mick always kept his first wage slip and a copy of this is now displayed in the historic display in reception at Simonstone.

Bill Foulds was another stalwart, an older man than us. He was a member at Burwain – he used to run the bar, as well as sail. His business in textiles had hit hard times and he had asked if there might be work available with us. Bespectacled and with not much hair remaining, Bill worked in a brown smock and wore clogs with steel toe-caps and irons on the soles – a remnant of his days in the mill. He worked downstairs and looked after stores and assembly. He also kept the younger lads in check with his conscientious and authoritarian demeanour.

One of Bill's tasks was to test the valves once assembled. This involved a 50 gallon drum full of paraffin, a rig to mount the valve and a pump to increase the pressure to around 50 p.s.i.. This pressure would reveal any leaking valve seal issues. Unfortunately, leaks did occur occasionally and, sometimes, spectacularly, covering Bill in paraffin. He would appear upstairs, a sorry sight, and have to go home to change. This took time and Fort the taskmaster came up with a solution. I bought Bill a sou'wester and oilskin coat for protection (and to save him leaving for an hour out of the working day, of course).

Bill also remained with us for many years. Most sadly, he became a casualty in a time of hardship at the company when we had to reduce staff levels. It was indeed so sad as he was such a dedicated man but he was 74 years old and he had to give way to the younger lads who we had to bring on. As I gave him the bad news he was in tears. He couldn't believe that he would be one of those to be leaving. "This is the worst day of my life," he said. I felt that. It has stayed with me.

On a more positive note, it was at Norfolk Street that we set on our first apprentice, Graham Johnson. He too has stayed with us, serving the company in many and varied positions for over 47 years. He was the first of many and it has always been most rewarding to give young starters in the industry a good grounding and encouragement. It is a fair return for my own apprenticeship at Rolls Royce all those years ago that defined my path and direction in life. My hope is that they might all be successful too. It is with tremendous satisfaction that I see that some prior apprentices are now at director level at Fort Vale.

How Graham joined us is an interesting tale. He was an apprentice at Bristols, working in Sough Bridge Mill (another coincidence). I had heard that the company was ceasing to operate and rang their office to see if they had any likely lads working as apprentices. They said they had and thought Graham might be suitable for us. They let me have his address in Foulridge, where he lived with his parents, and round I went. It was all very 'hands-on' in those days. His mother came to the door and I asked to see Graham, had a quick chat with him and was satisfied he was the right man to set on as an apprentice with us. He remembers to this day the exact date that he started – 19th May 1969. He also remembers the graft involved in the Colditz Shift.

Our labour force in those days came from several different and varied sources. Friends from the sailing club pitched in when they needed some work. Nigel Harris was with us on the shop floor for some time and introduced us to Burnley Light Alloys, the metal casting company who we continued to use for years. Later, John Hartley would work in his school holidays on labouring duties, machining adapters or deburring cast iron valve bodies – whatever was needed, even red-leading the bolt heads on the asbestos roof of the works. (Health and Safety would have been appalled.) Later still, we were joined by ex-Bradford University sailor, Brian Thomas, who stayed for many years.

These informal, and more formal, appointments supplemented the more usual procedures of press advertising and interview as well as word of mouth contacts for skilled and semi-skilled men.

Another address I went to in search of a conscript was that of Clive

Left: Skelton Street Works, Colne. The original Norfolk Street premises can be seen at the bottom of the street

Price. He was out of work, I knew, but was well respected. His wife answered the door and, when I had explained my presence, she shouted through to the back, "Clive, there's someone here to see you."

"I'm busy," I heard coming from the back room as a reply.

"It's about a job," his wife persisted.

"I'm still busy." This did not go down too well with Mrs. Price who disappeared down the hallway. Shortly afterwards, Clive appeared and, after a short interview on the doorstep, I asked him to join us, and he agreed. He started the next morning. Clive stayed with the company for 42 years until his retirement. I am so proud of having these long-serving colleagues. It convinces me that we do look after our workforce. Fort Vale would not be where it is today if it were not for so many loyal employees.

The name 'Fort Vale', by the way, was created by brother Robert. The origin of 'Fort' is obvious but 'Vale'? The town of Colne is situated on a hill. It is a very old town, preceding the expansion of the industrial revolution period by centuries. It is far older than some of the towns born purely from the growth of the textile industry, such as nearby Nelson. 'Bonnie Colne on the Hill' is a well-known local phrase. On either side of the town are the North and South Valleys. Norfolk Street lies towards the bottom of the hill in the North Valley and this inspired Robert to add the word Vale to the company name. It adds a little more character in a way, is more memorable and rolls off the tongue. It has certainly stood the test of time. At one point a change of name was considered but rejected as the existing name was so well known and respected in the industry. The only issue is an occasional confusion with the football team, Port Vale.

Mr Clive Price,

Nelson,

Lancs.

11 – 12 – 2012

Dear Ted & Ian,

      I am writing to thank you for my retirement gift. I feel like a lord wearing it. I have never had anything worth this much in my whole life and I will treasure it for the rest of my days. I will then pass it on to my children. In some ways Ted I was glad that you couldn't be there on the morning that I retired, because I would have found it too emotional. I always liked and admired you even when we didn't see eye to eye about things (seems that was on most things) But you gave me a job when no else would, and for that I will always be grateful. I would like to close by wishing you and your families a MERRY CHRISTMAS & HAPPY NEW YEAR. All the best to you both for the future.

Yours sincerely

Clive

Above: Clive Price's very kind note to Ian Wilson and myself on his retirement

We were growing ever faster and the inevitable happened. We were desperately short of space and we could dig ourselves no more. Just up the street from our current workshops was a printing works. It had more space and being so close would act as extra shop floor without having to interrupt production at Norfolk Street too much. Located on Skelton Street it also had more in the way of office space, which was also becoming more desperate.

I was in the middle of negotiations with the printer and about to complete the deal when another character turned up. He had travelled down from Windermere and immediately announced that he was the landlord of the property. The printer, it turned out, was a complete rogue and was about to sell me a building that he did not own!

The simple move up the street to Skelton Street Mill was fairly smooth and the extra space was much appreciated by all. We had about five Dufil machines by this time, as well as other equipment, and had started a night shift. Graham Johnson became night shift supervisor and was the best man we had at the challenging position. I used to call in, unannounced, at two o'clock in the morning to check that all was running smoothly.

Another milestone – our first female employee joined the company – Christine Hindle. We were in dire need of someone to maintain the administration functions in the office. We interviewed and I remember Christine saying that she did not change jobs very often. That was an understatement as she worked with us for over forty years until she retired in 2015. She did start, however, on a two weeks temporary cover, supplied by an agency. It was her first office post and she was most surprised when Robert and I came into the office from the shop floor and introduced ourselves. We had oil-stained white coats and shook her hand with our rather grubby ones. She went home, apparently, full of her new position and the fact that the company boss got his hands dirty and "…actually worked for a living".

She later reminded me of some of the lighter moments at Skelton Street – decorating the offices – herself and ourselves – over a weekend: the cat, which caught mice in the stores but which Robert hated. She also mentioned a pet hate – having to walk to the offices of Foluco Design, an associate company set up later, in order to send a telex (remember those?). Their office was a good fifteen minutes walk away. Poor Christine. "God, I must have been fit in those days," she remarked.

Another episode was when I arrived at the office with Jeeves, our boisterous black Newfoundland. As I opened the door, Jeeves raced in, excited and bouncy, leapt up onto Christine's desk and slid across the surface, wiping every item off and landing on the floor, where he looked pleased with himself, tail wagging furiously. I had to laugh – but Christine did not.

Through all these early years of business I was still enjoying life. Business was rewarding when achieving a success but I would not say it was always fun. Sailing was fun and I was still happy racing the Firefly at Burwain, visiting Abersoch and National Championships. Somehow, though, I could not put down business. To me, life is a total mixture – I cannot separate one aspect from another: it's as the warp and the weft in the weave of cloth. I will always have a business card to pass on to a prospective contact in industry, whether at the golf course or sailing club. When away at a sailing event I will have looked up which companies nearby were in our market area. I would contact them and arrange a visit before or after sailing. On holiday I am the same. You never know when a coincidence might throw up an opportunity. I saw it, and still see it, as one way of maximising potential.

We got into the export market in exactly this way.

Chapter 8

Sailing to Success

I have always sailed. From the earliest adventures with David Huggins at Silecroft and St. Annes, sailing has always been an intricate part of my life. I say 'intricate' because business life, social life and sailing have been interwoven and inseparable throughout. To repeat the weaving analogy, if business was the warp of life, then sailing was the weft.

In 1971 the Firefly national championships were being held at Dun Laoghaire, Ireland, hosted by the Royal St. George Sailing Club. I organised the logistics for a group of us to travel over for the event on a minimal budget. The logistics called for some clever shipping arrangements, only made possible by the proximity of the sailing club in Ireland to the ferry terminal.

The plan was for myself to travel out a couple of days early – on business of course – towing my own boat and also carrying a total of four masts on the trailer. The remaining Fireflies were to rendezvous at the ferry terminal in Holyhead and transfer all the boats onto one car and trailer combination, with the crews travelling as car or foot passengers. In this way, we could minimise the cost of the ferry crossing.

Right: The rest of the team load up for the ferry to Ireland.

l to r: Robin Delves, Max Uttley, Chas Ingham, Peter Richards, John Hartley, Nigel and Roger Harris. The children are Susan and Richard (sitting) Delves

Those in the team were Roger and Nigel Harris; Chas Ingham (from Royal Windermere Yacht Club) and Max Uttley; John Hartley crewing for me and Robin Delves with Peter Richards, currently commodore at SCYC (2015-6).

Robin Delves' Austin 1800 was put to the test. Two boats were tied to the trailer – one upside down on top of the other. A third was lifted onto the roof of the car, well padded, upside down again, and strapped on as best the boys could manage. Launching trolleys too had to be accommodated. It must have been quite a sight to see this rocky assembly carefully crawling up the ramp to the car deck, with an escort of crewmen walking alongside, supporting the upper hulls to prevent them from falling off.

Remarkably the boats made it across the Irish Sea without incident. At the port in Dun Laoghaire, the reverse procedure saw the boats separated and placed on their own trolleys for the short walk over to the sailing club dinghy park. Here they were reunited with the masts and myself.

John and Peter were only young at the time and before we left England, I had to ask John's father for approval before he would be allowed on the trip. His father (later to become commodore at Burwain) was a congregationalist of a local Methodist church. Our conversation was rather one-sided. "Look here, Ted" he began, "I've heard all about you young lads and your exploits." I knew exactly what he meant and said nothing.

"John can go with you but only on the proviso that you look after him and he must not join in your drinking sessions." I gave my assurances, trying to appear humble and contrite. As it turned out, John was a quick learner and soon held his own in the scheme of things. Of this group and as mentioned earlier, Nigel Harris worked at Norfolk Street for a while in the very early days, as did John Hartley in his school holidays, cycling along the canal path from his home in Brierfield every day.

I had not been idle in my first week in Ireland – warp and weft. It was a business trip (which meant it could be part funded by an expense account) and I had a particular contact in Dublin that I was keen, nay determined, to track down. Tom Barry was a former senior manager of the Esso Company who ran a parts supply business for the road tanker industry. I knew his name but not his contact details. I had to track him down, like some TV detective. I finally got his address from the Esso offices and, at the very end of the day, at around 5 or 6 o'clock at night, Tom Barry opened his front door to an exhausted young man – and took pity.

"You look done-in. You'd better come inside." Tom was a charming man. He did not know me from Adam and even when I introduced myself as a manufacturer and supplier, Fort Valve Engineering meant nothing to him. All the same, he made me a very welcome cup of tea.

After a long and convivial conversation, I had my first export order – he would take ten 3-inch BSP dustcaps at the value of ten pounds – or was it ten punts? (I can't remember.) Not ten pounds each – ten pounds for the total order but there it was, another pivotal moment, the first ever export order and taken on a sailing trip: warp and weft – and so it's always been. Tom became our agent in the Republic for AD tanker equipment and we had a wonderful friendship, working together for many years.

Ireland was to be the location of one more pivotal moment in Fort Vale history, perhaps the most important of all in defining the future direction of the Company's product range and its growth.

A little later after we had been sailing in Ireland, Stuart Lowley was exhibiting at an exhibition at Ryland Tankers in Birmingham. Rylands made road tankers and would invite their customers to see their range of tankers but also suppliers to show their supporting equipment at the event. Stuart was selling our range for AD tankers – the nozzles, three-way valves and the rest. A company from Ireland, CPV of Clones, visited the stand and saw the handnuts that we supplied for fastening down manlids on the tankers. They had a requirement for these handnuts for use on the new ISO Tank Containers that were beginning to become popular in the transportation of liquids. We visited their factory and began a trading relationship in this emerging and exciting market area.

The ISO Tank Container was totally new at the time. It is common now, of course, as are the box containers which can be seen stacked high on the decks of ships bringing in goods from, and exporting to, locations around the world in huge quantities. The ISO initials (International Standards Organisation) refer to the standardisation

Right: The Fort Vale exhibition stand at the Ryland Tankers exhibition 1972

Left: Stacks of ISO Tank Containers. The stainless steel manlid, relief valves and flow control valves are all Fort Vale products

of the dimensions of the tank frame, which use the same handling and securing points as the box containers. The design was developed by Bob Fossey, an engineer who worked for Williams Fairclough in London. He produced a swap body tank for transport on both road and rail in 1964, which was then manufactured to the ISO standards in 1967. It was revolutionary in the transport of liquids as they were previously shipped in drums for maritime shipping or road tankers. Drums were not efficient in the cargo to volume ratio and vehicular road tankers could not be shipped without handling the entire vehicle or trailer. The Tank Container carried more cargo per vessel volume and could be shipped easily by the existing cranes and infrastructure of container ports.

The market expanded at a remarkable rate and, likewise the demand for associated equipment – valves, manlids and more. By 2015 there were around 444,220 Container Tanks in use around the world. The majority of these would be using Fort Vale equipment. Fort Vale manufactures around 22,000 sets of tank container equipment per year. In 2014, 48,200 new tanks were manufactured – a figure that is increasing year on year (as of 2015).

Following our visit to CPV in Ireland, they made a return visit to Colne. Colin Boyle from the company had orders for tanks but was struggling to find a valve suitable for use on them. "I want valves," he said. "I just want some valves." But it was not just that simple.

He needed a completely new design that was possible to fit to the tanks within the ISO framework but still function well. The volume of the tank vessel had to be maximised within the framework leaving limited room for appendages such as valves. And these tanks were manufactured in stainless steel, another specialist requirement as the valves would have to be too. He needed Fort Vale. Our ability to react quickly to produce a new design, coupled with our knowledge of liquids handling provided the solution with an original and efficient design for a stainless steel footvalve – the valve at the bottom of the tank through which the liquid cargo is emptied. The larger valve manufacturing companies could never have responded as quickly or as effectively.

A further advantage that we had came from our knowledge of airflow. The Tank Container, like all vessels, has an emergency relief valve atop the tank. This relieves pressure in the event of a fire, say, when contents might expand at such a rate as to cause an explosion if pressure is not relieved. A pressure cooker blowing off steam illustrates the point.

Below: The Maxi Highflow pressure-vacuum relief valve which was a revolutionary design

Similarly, a vacuum needs to be relieved. A vacuum is formed if a tank's contents are discharged. Normally, a manlid might be opened on top of the tank to let air in as the tank is emptied but this may be overlooked. Air pressure is a powerful force. If a vacuum is allowed to be created in a tank, the atmospheric pressure acting on the tank from outside will crush the tank as easily as you would a fizzy drinks can.

The knowledge and experience I had gained from the time spent on the airflow test rigs at Lucas Aerospace became invaluable. We already had a Twinact relief valve used on road tankers but the Tank Container required a much higher rate of airflow than anyone had ever achieved previously. I developed the Maxi Highflow relief valve to an extremely high level of detail in terms of surface profile, poppet lift, spring performance and other areas within the required dimensions and parameters to achieve the required flow. The valve became the industry standard as its high performance meant that one Maxi Highflow per tank replaced the three or four standard valves needed previously.

Had it not been for taking that 7/6d bet when working at Rolls Royce, another decision made as a joke, which resulted in my joining Lucas in the first place, this landmark valve design would never have been possible. The slightly ironic point about these early days of the relief valve is that we had to take the design to my old employer, Lucas Aerospace, for flow testing before we had our own test facility. I was very, very nervous about approaching Lucas myself, having previously left the company: I had to leave it to others to make contact and organise the arrangements for the testing. A further irony is that the

Left: On board "Fly Fred" on Windermere with brother Robert and his wife, Joanna, and Kathleen Bedford

test procedure at Lucas was found to be wanting when inspected by our customer, Sea Containers. The results of the tests were too optimistic. This was remedied and the valve design was refined to perform to the required standards. Later, tests took place at British Gas at enormous expense, £20,000 for a morning, hastening further the development of our own test facility.

This initial introduction to exporting via the trade with CPV and to what was to be a major growth market for the company, the tank container market, all stemmed from the initial sailing trip to the Firefly Nationals in Ireland. Business and sailing were rather too closely associated in one incident that championship week. I was attempting to explain the advantages of a stirrup pump we sold to a potential customer when he demanded a practical demonstration. I thought quickly and decided that a demonstration would be possible in my hotel bedroom where there was a bath. We went up to the room only to find Mr. Delves still in bed, recovering from the previous night's excesses. I ignored his presence totally, as though it was a normal situation and continued with the demonstration in the bathroom, with

Delves snoring away in the background. Not at all professional, I'm afraid but enthusiasm took over from logic.

Charles Ingham, who was with us in Ireland, encouraged my joining his sailing club, the Royal Windermere Yacht Club at Bowness. The time had come for me to move up to a larger boat and at the RWYC they had started to sail the three-man racing keelboat, the Soling class. This was a Danish design and in 1968 had been selected as an Olympic class for the 1972 Munich Games. I was attracted by the way the boat handled and with the competitiveness of the class and bought one – number K59. That number which seemed to pop up in life so often did it again. At Windermere I met Graham Murray who also sailed Solings. Graham was a dentist, practicing in Harrogate who – and this is another coincidence – was in the same University of Leeds sailing team as John Hartley in the early seventies. We had a spell in the Flying Fifteen class of boat – Graham could always beat me in those – but it was the Soling that appealed more.

I really enjoyed the racing against Charles, Graham and others on Lake Windermere and from there we travelled to many regattas and open meetings around the country and in Europe before venturing further afield and to Bermuda for Race Week. First, though, I had to become more accomplished and sought out a better location in terms of sailing conditions than Lake Windermere. As pleasant an area as it was, the lake was flanked by high hills which made wind conditions erratic. The narrowness of the lake also was not ideal. A larger and more competitive fleet was based in Scotland on the Clyde and it was to the Royal Gourock that I moved the boat. I travelled there on a regular basis, sailing with Richard Burhouse, another ex-Bradford University sailor from Burwain most weekends if we were not at an event elsewhere.

It was during this period of total commitment and extreme effort – both in the business and in achieving my sailing objectives – that my life was brought back into focus: back to reality with a sudden and unexpected wake-up call.

Chapter 9

New Life for Old Mills

In 1974, within months of each other, my mother and father died. It was completely unexpected. They were not old by today's standards, only in their sixties. Suddenly, the bedrock of family life was removed. It left a huge void.

Father went first. That day I had travelled down with Richard Burhouse to a Soling regatta at Burnham on Crouch. We went into the clubhouse and I was met almost immediately by one of the Officers, "Are you Mr. Fort?" When I said that I was, he said, "There has been an emergency Police message on the radio. Would you please telephone this number straight away." I was informed, over the phone, that my father had suffered a severe heart attack and I should return home as a matter of urgency. I drove straight back, crying all the way, only to find out when I got home that he was dead. That very afternoon, before I left for the weekend, I had taken afternoon tea with him and everything had been fine. He was 68 years old.

Mother never got over the loss and nine months later she too succumbed, aged 67.

It made me appreciate more than ever the huge part they had played

Left: Mother, Father and Robert – ever supportive, all

in defining and directing my route in life. Mother, who had always had faith in my ability, in spite of a less than encouraging academic performance, had arranged my extra tuition and apprenticeship. Father, ever supportive, from fetching black market rations during the war by bicycle from the farm at Pateley Bridge to delivering parts and supplies at Norfolk Street, never failed. He was described by Christine Hindle as "a lovely, kindly gentleman".

The foundations of my domestic life had gone, too. No longer could I rely on a meal being ready or clean shirts appearing without my considering from where. Wherever in the country sailing or business had taken me, I had a warm and reliable home with an attentive mother to which to return. No longer.

Having been so carefully looked after all my life, I was hopeless at looking after myself. I could not cook, as proved on "Sinbad" and lacked all other domestic skills. I did hire domestic help – I had to do – but it was never the same again. I think it was probably from this point onwards that I was looking for someone to fill that gap in my life. Finding someone with the dedication to look after my wellbeing, with the commitment that my mother had shown, was never likely to be possible. I had become used to being the centre of attention and having demands met. Some would say that I expect the same still.

In hindsight, I wonder if it was the need to fill this void that hastened the thought of marriage. I am not sure: it may have influenced things.

Throughout this entire period of change I was also pursuing a goal of being selected for the British sailing team to go to the Olympic games. I travelled widely with the Soling to all the events that counted towards selection. Initially, this involved travelling to Scotland each weekend.

It was in Scotland that I met my future wife, Fay Paterson. Romance blossomed that year after we met at sailing dinners and social occasions around the Clyde. We saw more and more of each other and tied the

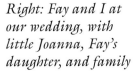

Right: Fay and I at our wedding, with little Joanna, Fay's daughter, and family

knot on March the 27th, 1975, at Southwick Church, not far from the coast on the Solway Firth where her family lived.

Very soon afterwards it became obvious that in order to reach a performance of Olympic standard in the Soling fleet I would have to start to compete in regattas held at sailing clubs on the south coast. The level of sailing in the south was higher and it was definitely the place to improve standards. What this meant, though, was a lot more travelling.

Every Friday, following a week's hard work, I would motor down to the Hamble, to Calshot for winter training or a sailing event in Weymouth, perhaps. Every weekend. I know not how we did it. At Calshot, staying at the RAF base where the sailing was centred, we had to sign in to get a bedroll, tin mug and cutlery for the weekend! Who said it was a glamorous sport? A long drive back to Lancashire on Sunday evening was necessary for me to be at work on Monday morning.

I sold Lancashire Ghyll after I was married and moved to the Old Vicarage in Read. Brother Robert moved into the family-owned farm of Higher Hague, a couple of fields above Lancashire Ghyll. He lived there with wife, Joanna and children, Peter and Hannah, until he tragically died in 2002. He is buried next to Mother and Father in the graveyard at Kelbrook Church, in true 'Fort Country' – the village with so many historic family connections.

Then I bought an old textile mill in Nelson. Yes, 1974 was a year full of surprises, some better than others. The purchase of Parkfield Mill was another of those coincidences, those lucky breaks, and another pivotal moment. From the grapevine network of the old textile industry came word that David Nelson, son of the famous textile giant, Amos

Nelson, had gone into receivership. It happened that the accountants acting for the Nelsons were a company called Proctor and Proctor. They also acted for the Kelbrook Mill Company, where we have family involvement from the days of Great-Grandfather, who was on the original board of directors.

Peter Baldwin from Proctors knew I might be interested and telephoned me to let me know that the mill was for sale. If it had not been for his telephone call, I would never ever have known that it was on the market and would have missed this golden opportunity for expansion. As it was, I had to move quickly. At a Colne pub that was a popular venue for local businessmen, I overheard a discussion about the purchase of a mill in Nelson and it was Parkfield. They seemed keen to proceed and one of the men I knew to be well-heeled enough to conclude the deal without a problem. I managed to finalise the deal and make the purchase quickly before anyone else could leapfrog me.

Compared to Norfolk Street and Skelton Street, Parkfield Mill was huge. It had a vast weaving shed on a single level with traditional cast iron pillars supporting a north light roof – the normal arrangement for a weaving shed. Attached to this was a two storey building with wonderful timber floors used as offices, storage, inspection and other functions involved in the trade. All the walls were faced in the locally-quarried, dressed stone, as were all the textile mills of that era.

Below: Parkfield Mill is the area with rows of north light roofing and the double pitch roof adjoining. The waste land to the right is where the demolished section of the mill once stood

A further weaving shed on a lower ground level, as large as the upper shed, had been demolished in the 1950's to cash in the scrap metal in the columns and troughings (the vernacular for rain gutters) for a couple of thousand pounds during a period of hardship. This large area of the site remained as derelict land.

But the place was huge. Although excellent value for money after negotiating with the Receiver, it was still an enormous commitment. These were times of uncertain and tense banking circumstances and I was not confident enough to move the company in immediately. We bought the mill in 1974 but did not occupy it until 1976.

Parkfield Mill had a rich and varied history spreading back over one hundred years. The mill was built in 1898 by Mr Edward Carr (informally known as "Teddy") who lived in Langroyd Hall, Colne. Fred Wainman & Co Limited commenced business at the mill in 1899 with 970 looms to weave cloth. By sheer coincidence it was discovered that Mr Wainman lived at Scholfield House, not far from the mill, and Ian Wilson, the Fort Vale Managing Director lived there as a boy.

Life was very hard in Nelson in 1898, the mills were lit by gas light and hours of work were 6 a.m. to 6 p.m., five days a week plus Saturday morning: this came to a total of 55 hours, with wages at £1 per a week. Children aged 10 years and above worked part time before school and after, with the school leaving age at 14. This was not raised to the age of 15 years until 1947.

The noise of the looms in the weaving sheds was deafening and drowned out all other sound, so spoken communication was impossible. Lip reading developed and very successful it was too. Although no

Above: The date, 1994, refers to the building of an office extension at Parkfield Works

Left: Queen Street Mill in Burnley is a preserved example of a typical Lancashire weaving shed

longer necessary, traces of the practice are evidenced in the unusually exaggerated articulations of mouth, lips and facial gestures still seen in mill towns today. The comedian, Les Dawson, mimicked this well.

I have always been impressed with the achievements of the industrial revolution. The working conditions left a lot to be desired, it is true, but then again the income of workers was improved, housing too. The wealth created enabled a solid local infrastructure to be established, illustrated by the growth of the transport networks, sewerage systems, water supplies, councils and town halls, etc. I like to think that the wealth I have managed to generate is put to good use in similar vein. We have the Fort Vale Apprenticeship scheme and my two charities aimed at providing a helping hand to local youngsters and a chance for them to succeed as well. I am a strong believer that with wealth comes responsibility.

It was the opening of the railway in 1849 that accelerated matters, with the population of Nelson increasing in the second half of the nineteenth century – from 6,068 in 1851 to 44,045 in 1901. New mills were constructed, and the introduction of the room and power system (where a mill was built, steam engine and driving gear installed, and then leased out to anyone who needed space for looms) in the area in 1857 caused an enormous increase in the number of looms and thus the number of workers required. In the 1860s and 1870s, over two thousand terraced houses were built, along streets laid out on a gridiron plan.

Some weavers flourished under the system, and went on to open up their own mills and rent space to other manufacturers. One such was James Nelson who had begun by renting space. He went on to own the largest weaving venture in Nelson, Valley Mills next to the Walverden Stream at Clover Hill. In the period between 1871 and 1914, there were thirty mills working in Nelson.

Below: A hot air balloon displays at "Jimmy's" social club sports ground

The Nelson family were philanthropic and established a social club for employees and their families. They built a large clubhouse with sports grounds in honour of the workers who fell in the First World War. It was well used for decades, popularly known as "Jimmy's", the classic building fell into disrepair and was demolished, sadly, in 2013.

Many of the weaving sheds and mills were cleared in the latter part of the twentieth century, particularly in the centre of town. Those that survived tend to lie on the outskirts of the town. Nelson's mills are characterised by the predominance of weaving rather than spinning, and therefore comprise single-storey weaving sheds extending over large areas.

By 1924 when the final two mills were built on green field sites there were over 50,000 looms in the weaving sheds of Pendle.

The textile industry began to decline in the 1920's and 30's. Some mills became empty or were populated by newer industries.

Engineering skills had always been required to install and maintain the machines in the weaving sheds – the engines, power drives, the looms themselves and all the ancillary equipment – so engineering as an industry with markets outside the textile industry began to develop. The core skills of the workforce adapted well to this.

'Shadow factories' was a plan developed by the British Government to implement additional manufacturing capacity for the British aircraft industry in the build up to World War II. When many of the traditionally industrial areas of Britain were under threat from the Luftwaffe's bombing raids and a further increase in output was required to meet the demands of war, production was duplicated in more remote locations. They were also employed for the later Korean conflict.

We were fortunate in our area, as previously we did not have much manufacturing industry. Several mills were taken over as 'shadows'. Wellhouse Mill in Barnoldswick was a huge factory well placed in the countryside. Other noted factories taken over at this time were Ghyll House and Fern Bank Mills, Barnoldswick, the Lucas complex in Burnley, and our own Parkfield Works in Nelson.

In 1940 the heavy raids on Coventry triggered the removal of the Rover Company's war production to the area. They took over five sheds as 'shadow factories' in Barnoldswick/Earby as well as Waterloo Shed at Clitheroe.

One section in Bankfield Shed at Barnoldswick housed an experimental unit run by Frank Whittle which became the birth place

Left: Sough Bridge Mill in Kelbrook, a 'shadow factory' in World War II. Grandfather, Sagar Fort, was on the Board of Directors of the owners, the Kelbrook Mill Company

of the jet engine made by Rolls Royce – and this is where I started my own career in engineering, in 1952 at the age of fifteen.

Sough Bridge Mill, near Kelbrook, was another of these. Due to our family connections with the Kelbrook Mill Company, I was asked to join the board of directors. On asking for the job guide for the position, I received a letter declining my appointment. They had been put out at my suggestion that one should actually perform as a director. They were used to merely turning up at each AGM to receive their remuneration.

In 1942 Rolls Royce swapped Rover a tank factory, gaining the jet engine works at Barnoldswick and Clitheroe. There was a historic handover when Rolls Royce gained the rights to manufacture the Whittle gas turbine engine. The handover is said to have taken place over a five-bob dinner at the Swan and Royal Hotel in Clitheroe when Ernest Hives of Rolls Royce said to S.B. Wilkes of Rover, "Why are you playing around with this jet engine? It's not in your line of business". Wilkes had not got a good relationship with Frank Whittle and was probably glad of the exchange. The truth of this episode is not assured as it is only as recounted by Sir Stanley Hooker some time later and is subject to continuing debate.

This factory was then mainly used for the manufacture of prototype engines and type testing the Merlin engine. The name RB211 given to the famous commercial jet engine comes from the initials of Rolls of Barnoldswick. Rover retained the other mills including Sough Bridge largely for work on building and refurbishing piston engines. These Rover concerns stayed until 1945 when they moved back to concentrate production in Coventry.

After the Second World War, in 1946/7, my grandfather had to pay betterment charges of £47,000 (£1.5m today) to get back Sough Bridge Mill for the Earby Mill Company, causing a great hoo-hah in the family.

The area was left with the advantages of converted mills suitable for engineering, a housing stock and a skilled work force but with very little work for them to do, apart from that at Rolls Royce in Barnoldswick. Wage rates were very low and the area was thus very attractive for incoming manufacturers. It was the most attractive prospect in the West Riding (Barnoldswick was still in Yorkshire at that time). In 1945/46 the company Armoride moved from Brighouse into Grove Mill at Earby and Bristol Tractors moved from Idle at Bradford into Sough Bridge. They recruited local labour that had no problem in converting from aero engine work to general engineering. Bristol were a company belonging to the Jowett car company and produced tracked vehicles until 1970 when they went bankrupt.

This influx and the existence of the small independent service firms spawned by the aero engine industry was the trigger for the transformation of the area from single-industry textile work to a wide industrial base founded on precision engineering.

As mentioned already, during the Second World War Parkfield Mill was requisitioned by the Government. After the war, in the 1950's, David Nelson took over the business and still used the premises as a textile mill until he went bankrupt and I bought them.

Our Works Manager at the time was the usually happy, unflappable Maurice Worsnop. I took him to see our new premises, the old Parkfield Mill. As we gazed on the immense area of shop floor, the look on his face, now pale, with a cigarette drooping from the corner of his mouth, said it all: we had an enormous task ahead of us. Nevertheless, with sterling work by the whole team and particularly Robert and Frank Hall with the wiring and installation, by September 1976 we were established and in production.

Frank had been made redundant as the Burnley branch of Websters, then Philips, had closed. This gave him the push he needed to set up his own electrical business and it was a good job for me that he did. Frank and Robert installed and commissioned all the machines in the works and also a backup generator.

Previously, Frank and Robert had built the generator in an old mill in Colne over a Christmas period, to keep the machines running in Skelton Street and enable production to meet demand during the Three-Day Week crisis. This was one of several measures introduced in the United Kingdom by the Conservative Government 1970-1974 to conserve electricity, the production of which was severely limited due

Left: Parkfield Works, Brunswick Street, Nelson

Above: The shop floor at Parkfield Works, c.1980.
l to r: Maurice Worsnop, Works Manager, Eric Smith, Chief Inspector, with brother, Robert. The manlid cover is of the old, fabricated type, prior to the later, pressed design

to industrial action by coal miners. The effect was that from 1 January until 7 March 1974 commercial users of electricity would be limited to three specified consecutive days' consumption each week and prohibited from working longer hours on those days.

Parkfield Works always had a warm feeling about it and Fort Vale occupied the building until 2008 when the last of the staff moved to the new facility in Simonstone. It was demolished in 2011 but the 'Turret' (a folly built from masonry from the mill) and 'Stonehenge' (an arrangement of the engine bed stones) were preserved in recognition of the achievements of the industrial revolution.

Stone has since become quite a passion of mine and has resulted in my collecting recovered masonry from old Lancashire buildings. I then take delight in reconstructing various garden features and 'follies', if you like, in and around our homes and grounds, both in Lancashire and Hampshire. I put it down in part to my desire to leave a legacy as well as an appreciation of the material itself.

The collection is mainly from the Lancashire area of my roots and includes stone from churches of St. John's and Brunswick Street in Nelson, Colne Baptists and Chatburn Methodists Chapels. The old church buildings were either too expensive to maintain with the

Left: Another view of the shop floor at Parkfield Works showing the assembly and testing areas with CNC machine tools in the background

dwindling coffers of a reducing congregation or surplus to requirements following amalgamations of churches close by each other. St. John's suffered from dry rot and was demolished in 1983/4. Chatburn, too, had terminally rotten timbers and was replaced by a new chapel on the same site later.

Far left:: three stalwart workers – Mick Meehan (left) who started at Norfolk Street, Clive Price (right) and Tim Hopkins who ran the stores at Parkfield Works. All three worked for me right up until they retired

Left: Levels of production grew at Parkfield Works. Here, butterfly valves are being assembled

Chapter 10

The Tank Container Market

By now, the business was expanding rapidly. I had realised that the ISO Tank Container market would be the defining way forward. On the 16th May, 1977, I sent the following memo to the management team…

CONTAINER TANK MARKET

From the report attached, you will see how important a market the Container Tank is for Fort Vale.

Without question we are market leaders in this field in our range of equipment that we can offer to the Tank Builders.

This must become 'OUR NO.1' product range and we must have:-

   a) The correct Machine Tools.

   b) Up-to-date designs.

   c) Test facilities.

   d) Comprehensive Tooling Programme.

   e) Sales Literature.

   f) Service Manual.

In other words we must tackle this as professionally as possible.

Signed:-

E. S. Fort

Right: The Tank Container market demand was rising all the time. Fort Vale became world leaders in the industry

Left: Maxi Highflow pressure/ vacuum relief valves became an industry standard and are made in huge quantities

We were creating new designs and levels of order were increasing with the growing popularity of the ISO tank container. New designs were the key to our success. We were finding ways of improving the performance of our products all the time, making sure that our competitors were always playing catch-up.

I took the details of the new Maxi Highflow valve to the U.S. Federal Register in Washington in order to get official approval, which would allow it to be fitted to tanks there. The valve would relieve the pressure built up in a tank when engulfed by fire, allowing expanding gases to escape and thus preventing the tank exploding in the heat. I presented the valve itself with test results and flow curves.

From there I visited the Chief Engineer of Dupont in Wilmington, Delaware, to discuss the performance of the valve. Holding the valve in my hand, I told him just how special this new valve was. "This valve has a CD of 0.94" I stated.

The engineer just smiled. A coefficient of discharge (CD) of 1.00 is a flow level through a valve (in this case) that does not impede the flow at all – impossible to achieve, of course. A CD of 0.94 through a valve with a lifting poppet (passing 94% of a full flow volume) is an extremely good figure and gives excellent performance.

"Mr. Fort," he said, "would you say that number again – slowly".

"0.94" I repeated. A pause for thought was followed by his response, "Are you God? No-one has ever made a valve like that before."

My knowledge of airflow test rigs from days at Lucas Aerospace had helped us to obtain exceptional results. The valve became a mainstream product for Fort Vale. Such was the degree of product development we were achieving through our talented design team – with my guidance, of course! In the last 15 years the company has manufactured some 320,000 Maxi Highflow valves. The latest relief valves made at Fort Vale today, such as those for the U.S. fracking oil rail car market, are based around the same basic principles and design guides.

I was reminded recently of another important landmark product when passing what were the offices of Sea Containers in London. They were major players in the tank container leasing business and, as such, a potentially huge customer for us. I managed to arrange a meeting with Managing Director, Preben Hansen, to present a new design for a butterfly valve. It was to be used to control the rate of flow of a product through the valve assembly at the bottom of a tank container. Previously this was achieved with a combination of a lifting-poppet footvalve (the on/off switch) and a large ball valve (the throttle). My new valve would have cleaner internal lines, be more compact and have improved flow rates. Unfortunately, I was struggling to find anyone in the design office to draw up the design with technical specifications: we were so busy on production that detailing drawings for manufactured parts had priority.

Finally I called upon one of John Hartley's staff, a young graphic designer called Ashley Pickard, to produce the drawings. John by this time was running Hartley & Hartley – a design and print company doing a lot of work for us in marketing. I set off for the meeting sure that the new design was going to change the industry – in its modest way. Hansen was convinced immediately and made the

Right: A modern valve assembly as fitted to the outlet flange of a tank container – a footvalve and butterfly valve combination

decision, on the spot, to change the specification on all his new orders for tank containers to replace the ball valves with our butterfly valve. Sea Containers became a major customer and the butterfly valve did become a new standard fitting in the industry. It and its many variations are still made in large quantities today.

These new product designs were rolling out of the design office quicker and quicker. A close association with customers and responding to their requests for improvements in performance or specification kept us at the forefront in terms of sales. The competition, and there were some other companies manufacturing in our market at the time, was finding it impossible to keep pace. Our manufacturing procedures, quality of materials and quality control, to reinforce our cutting-edge product design, gave us an excellent reputation in the industry. I have always said that one should never make a product that could bite back. A vacuum cleaner or motor car can fail. Our valves were solid and reliable. They were thoroughly tested and returns were next to zero.

Products should always be tested as they would be operated in service and I have always insisted that Fort Vale products are tested thoroughly. This came from my experience gained at Lucas Aerospace where testing was crucial. An example is the currently produced API coupler. An automatic test rig was designed and built by Graham Johnson. The rig tests the API valve with over 250,000 continuous operations, which involve connection, opening, closing and disconnection. This has set the industry standard and customers now require this level of testing.

In the ISO Tank Container industry, we had the respect of the regulatory body and were represented on their committee to give help and advice on safety and the feasibilities of product development.

This was all extremely beneficial to business but could backfire sometimes if we were perceived to be monopolistic. I can see why that may have occurred but we were always on the side of the customer – we knew that we had to maintain trust and confidence. We have always strived to maintain that philosophy.

The company was profitable – it had to be. Expansion can often drain resources and, if too rapid, will bring a company down. Money will simply run out. Cash flow problems are the most common causes of business failure. Professor Roland Smith reminded me that "You can run at a loss for years but you can only run out of money once."

At one point, I was approached by Tony Clegg, who was still running Drum, with a view to his buying Fort Vale. He had ideas of expansion and going public. With my strategy of running my own private company and not wanting shareholders, this was never going to happen, of course. I could not understand why some people wanted to go public. Tony did eventually set up a public company called Syltone (from Sylvia and Tony) but it cost a fortune even to simply administer.

Still, he profited personally from the exercise of course and bought a yacht, which is what he wanted.

A local friend and businessman, Tom Clarke, also went public with his company, Silentnight. "Why," I asked him, "did you go public?"

"I am getting on," he said, "and I wanted some capital to spend and enjoy life before it's too late. Once you reach three score years and ten, Fort, you're on borrowed time." He died in 1993 at the age of 74. Tom, too, was awarded the OBE for services to industry, as was I.

I needed to be making good profits as machine tools we were using at Fort Vale were undergoing huge technological advances, which were reflected in their price. They were becoming much more capable but, with that, more complicated and more expensive. I have never shirked from investing in the best equipment, though, if possible and practical – just as with that very first Harrison 17-inch lathe. Buying machines too small can be an error in the longer term. We continue to reinvest in a large proportion today – in machines, facilities, premises, and in people.

The team was growing. Key characters were Dave Smith in the design office and Bernard Ineson, the Sales Director and a former Drum employee, like me.

Dave Smith needs special recognition for his huge commitment to the company over many years – decades, in fact. His expertise has been crucial in so many ways in the development of new products and production techniques. It is not an exaggeration to say that without Dave, the company would not be where it is today.

As the name suggests, the ISO Tank Container market was global.

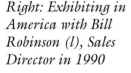

Right: Exhibiting in America with Bill Robinson (l), Sales Director in 1990

Just as with the box container, tank containers were transporting liquids around the world and accelerating the creation of the Global Market with which we are so familiar today. Tank manufacturing was global – they were being made in the UK, Ireland (CPV), South Africa and America but not particularly in China at this early stage. South Africa was the centre of most of the action.

So, of course, we had to travel. We had to let the world know who we were and that they really needed us on board in their manufacturing endeavours. Major trade exhibitions were held at various international locations periodically – perhaps twice a year. I had started to travel abroad with sailing – starting with that epic Irish trip – and had subsequently visited several countries with the Soling. I was getting used to travel and was enjoying it.

As an aside, the tax and expenses arrangements in those days were very different to today. If one was abroad for more than 65 days in the year, the income tax rate reduced dramatically – at one point it reduced it from 80% to 25%. Expenses were put through without question, unlike today when they are scrutinised to the nth degree.

Bernard and I started to travel the world. As well as the UK exhibitions – the Commercial Motor Show at Earls Court, later combined with the Motor Show at the NEC – we attended exhibitions from Monte Carlo to Houston and Singapore to Dubai: taking product samples and some display panels and literature. We had to be seen alongside the tank manufacturers, see their customers – they were our customers too. We joined the circuit, joined the club. Bernard was good at this side of things. He would major on the communication and networking and I preferred the business and technical portfolio – although Bernard was excellent on the technical too, it was just that I sometimes fell a little short on diplomacy.

Everyone knew everyone – it was a tight little industry – and everyone got on well, off the field of play, that is. We knew all the tank manufacturers and leasing companies well and were very involved in their products and services. Sometimes Bernard or I would be taken to one side and asked, quietly, perhaps over a beer, about another manufacturer's operations. We had to be extremely cautious and became expert at changing the subject. Our integrity and reputation remained intact, however boisterous the evening get-togethers became. We had come a long way from that first meeting with CPV at the exhibition held in the garage at Ryland Tankers in Birmingham.

It was paying off, though. The rate of increase of orders and turnover were fast accelerating but I realised that this needed control. I didn't want to trip over our success and fall flat. An improved, more structured management system needed to be installed and looked after. I needed a new man, a key player of the right calibre.

Chapter 11

Expanding the Business

I found myself increasingly short of time. With the realisation that I was moving the company to a higher level, it became obvious that I needed a manager of a high calibre to control our growth. After some consideration of alternatives, I contacted a headhunting company.

Ian Wilson came for interview on a Saturday morning. The appointment was for 10.00 a.m. at Parkfield Works. He was living in Bedford at the time but was staying with family in Blackpool for the weekend to facilitate the meeting. It turned out that he had been born in Nelson – yet one more amazing coincidence in life.

I expect he thought that the interview would last an hour or so, perhaps two. I thought the interview would last a couple of hours at most. I think I must have got rather carried away. We got on well and, following a tour of the shop floor, we discussed my plans for expansion, the world market, advancing technology and much more.

I gave Ian a small valve design problem to solve but this was not his forté, it turned out, when returning to study his designs. His talents lay in production administration – the exact area in which I needed help. The conversation continued through the day and in the end it was time for dinner! We went back to The Old Vicarage for dinner, where I introduced the family, plus dog, and we continued the conversation. Ian did not get back to his waiting wife until after midnight. He subsequently told me that his explanation for the late hour of his return seemed thin. Some interview.

Fortunately, Ian did join us and he still is at Fort Vale as the Managing Director. He came to the company in 1978, which was just before computers became more common in business. I am hopeless with computers – I can't use one at all and I don't try. As well as mastering and guiding the commercial operation of the company, Ian had grasped the new technology with enthusiasm. He bought our first ever computer and we still have it. It was a Commodore Pet 8k, bought as a familiarisation exercise. I am told that the 8k is the size of the RAM and that an electric toaster has more processing power these days. Still, what do I know? Actually, what do I need to know, more appropriately?

At the time of buying the first commercially useful computer, we had a report from a consultant that said that the company did not need one. Ian insisted that we did and that we spend £20,000 on a Nixdorf,

Below: Ian Wilson, Managing Director, Fort Vale Engineering Limited

Right: Anne Hartley joins me on the 'Turret' at Beaulieu

our first commercial system. They were so much more expensive in the early development years of computing than they are now. So I said to Ian, in very clear terms, "You do realise that you are putting your shirt on this new technology?" and that we would have to see how it worked out. I was sceptical. As it happened, of course, our computer system turned out to be a very effective secret weapon in the business.

Very quickly, Ian became familiar with the workings of the company. Through a combination of observation, talking with staff on all levels and studying the market and customer requirements, he identified strengths and weaknesses. He addressed both and very soon it became apparent that we had a most capable and hardworking addition to the team. My role became more strategic and Ian managed the majority of the commercial activities. We have only had a few differing opinions from time to time but over nothing that could not be rationalised. We have always got on well, one-to-one.

Anne Hartley joined us at this time as well – if only provisionally. Anne has become invaluable in the efficient way that she organises my diary, arrangements and the bulk of my business affairs. Her ability to read situations, react appropriately and keep me out of trouble – mostly – is remarkable. I said 'provisionally' because Anne joined us initially from an agency as a 'temp'. She worked as such for six months, very diligently, before asking whether it would be possible to have a permanent position. I said, "Of course", and, in my usual less-than-most-sensitive way, asked her in for an interview. Anne said

Below: The 8k Commodore PET, the starting point of the age of computing at Fort Vale

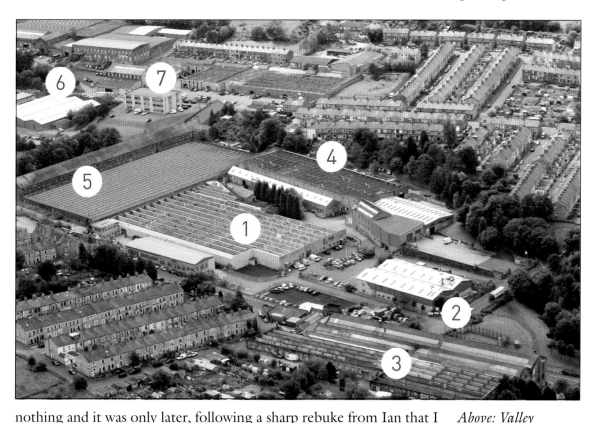

nothing and it was only later, following a sharp rebuke from Ian that I discovered that Anne had been quite upset to have to be interviewed for a job she had been fulfilling successfully for six months already. She illustrated her capacity to cope with my clumsiness, I am glad to say, as she remains a stalwart colleague to this day.

Again, with the expanding demands on production, we were pressed for space. A possible solution appeared on the horizon, a vacant mill nearby. Here was the legacy of the textile industry once more.

Parkfield Works (as we had renamed it from the textile-related word, 'Mill') was located above the South Valley and only a street or two from the edge of what once was the largest textile-manufacturing complex in Europe. The entire collection of mills had come up for sale – I had to have a look. Ian was worried that I may be over extending but it was clear to me that we needed more room.

The mills were part of the family business of the Nelson family (the same name as the town but only by co-incidence).

The founder, James Nelson became a handloom weaver in 1842 at the age of eleven, following the family tradition. He earned 1/6d a week at a mill in his home village of Winewall. Later he became an Overlooker and then at the age of 36, Mill Manager.

In 1881, when 50, he was faced with the problem of making a fresh

Above: Valley Mills, Nelson.
1 - No.1 shed - home to Riggs Autopack until their move to (6) in 2013
2 - Site of No.2 shed, now Fort Vale Foundry:
3 - No. 3 shed:
4 - No. 4 shed, occupied by Fort Vale Engineering for manufacturing:
5 - No. 5 shed, the DHSS national archive until 2015
6 - Premier Mill:
7 - Brunswick House, home of Hartley & Hartley until 2002

start in life. The weaving mill that he had managed for 14 years was closing down. His son, Amos, also had begun his career at an early age and by the time he was 21 he had worked in every department of a cotton mill and had saved £200 from his wages.

So these two, James aged 50 and Amos aged 21, decided to move to Nelson and there in Brook Street they rented space for 160 looms. By the end of the 1860s they had a total of 1000 looms, mostly at Walverden Shed. After a period of expansion, they decided to build their own mill. So, in 1895, No. 1 Mill at Valley Mills was completed and then, in 1899, No. 2 Mill. These were followed by Nos. 3 and 4 Mills, eventually becoming the largest weaving venture in Nelson.

In November 1946 James Nelson Ltd. became a public company under the Chairmanship of Sir Amos Nelson, as he now was. However, on the eve of the first Board Meeting of this new company in 1947 he died, after managing the affairs of the company for 66 years. He was succeeded by his second son, Mr. David R. Nelson.

James Nelson Limited was acquired by Courtaulds, who ran down the business in the 1980s and finally shipped the remaining production, including all the machinery, to Pakistan.

Sheds Nos. 1, 2, 3 and 4 of the complex were available to buy. The day these Valley Mills were put on the market by Courtaulds they were part of the 60 mills that they put on the market in one day. Shed 5, Valley Mills, housed Government records from 1947, 350 people worked there and there were 16 million files and 54 miles of shelving at its peak before it closed in 2015.

I well remember walking through the ranks of silenced looms when viewing the properties. They reminded me of the silent factory in Yeadon where I had put in an offer on those first two machines as a joke but which had been so instrumental in my early success. Now, here in Nelson, were row upon row of weaving warriors, regiments no longer banging and clattering as swords on shields: no more flying shuttles and with empty beams for warp. Warp and weft, eh? How times change.

Shed after shed, floor after floor they went on. It took over an hour to walk around and take it all in. It would not all be practical for our requirements, I decided: there were issues of different floor levels and awkward access. This complex of mills had grown organically, it was apparent, and had crawled up the valley sides in steps, which would not suit modern shop floor demands for efficient movements.

I considered our requirements very carefully and finally, in 1988, bought just No. 4 Shed and part of No. 1 Shed.

The Fort Vale Foundry was built on the site of No. 2 Shed, which had been demolished in the early 1990s prior to my obtaining the land on which it had stood.

Fort Vale owned five old textile mills in Nelson at one point in time, two of which were those of Sir Amos Nelson. Another common appreciation I have with Sir Amos Nelson is his love of good architecture. He commissioned a fine house, Gledstone Hall, near Skipton, from the famous architect, Sir Edwin Lutyens. It was built in the years 1923-26 on Sir Amos' 6,500 acre estate. It is a fine building in stone and has a block of stables that were built by German prisoners of the First World War. He employed four chauffeurs, residing in Southfield Street, Nelson, near his mills. His son, David, from whom we bought Parkfield Mill, continued to live at the house, converting the stables as his residence.

Above: The large press producing pressings for manlids

We moved several areas of production into No. 4 Shed, including the line making the new design of my pressed manlid. The manlid is a hinged cover of 18 or 20 inch diameter (460 or 500 mm these days) on the top of a tank giving access to the inside for inspection and cleaning. It seals on a neckring and is held down by several bolts with handnuts around the edge. Traditionally, the manlid had been fabricated from a dished plate dome and a cast outer ring. I came up with a revolutionary new design in pressed stainless steel for the manlid, with a huge saving in production costs. The way this came about was another of these 'pivotal moments' that keep appearing in my life.

In 1980 I was visiting an agricultural exhibition near Warwick. I saw a manlid on the back of a road tanker just like the ones we were making but in a flash, a single moment of inspiration, I had the idea to make it as a pressed manlid. With the brilliant jig and tool expertise of Dave Smith in the design office, we produced a market-leader. We got a world patent on our design in 1981 and we now manufacture 20,000 manlids per year: nobody has had the skill to copy our design.

Following on from this, when I visited the tank container manufacturers, Consani, in South Africa, I was given a hard time over the neckring supplied for the manlid. When it was lower in height, we charged more for it, as it was a lower volume item. I needed a solution. When I came back to Fort Vale I quickly drew up a new design for a swept neckring and Dave Smith, again, created the tooling for efficient production. We were the first company, I think, in the world to manufacture a pressed manlid and neckring.

We did need improved production machines to be able to meet the new manufacturing challenges of our improving range of products. Where the manlids were concerned, this included a new 200-ton press to achieve the required deflection of the necessary thickness of steel plate involved. Following lengthy discussions with Ian, I decided we had to have one and to push ahead with buying this expensive Goliath of a machine. Going into Ian's office I said, "Now Mr. Wilson, take

*Above:
Manufacturing
pressed manlids
in No. 4 shed*

a deep breath," and after he had, "and take another deep breath," he did, "and order it!" He did.

Advancements in production technology continued to be essential in all areas. A particularly rapidly advancing area that I became very aware of was the computer numerically controlled (CNC) machines. These were programmed to perform several operations on a component, including cutting tool changes. They were also being coupled with automatic loading and unloading facilities – the beginnings of the robot age.

I had, with Ian Wilson, seen these demonstrated at a manufacturer's premises and was convinced we could benefit from the technology. I placed an order. There was a level of resistance to buying robots from Ian, initially, stemming from a lack of knowledge of these new beasts and how they functioned. In fact, on the flight back, he said that we would cancel the order when we got home.

However, I called Ian into my office the next day and forcefully put the point that unless we did get one of these machines and use it, we would never know how they worked. I insisted that the technology was to be mastered and we now have armies of these efficient, precision machine tools. I call them my artillery in the battle with competition.

I meet resistance to the adoption of some new idea or technology from time to time. I always try to be first with new technology. I find it easy to see where a new machine technology, or any other key factor for that matter, will give us an advantage. Others may not, yet they do recognise that I can think 'outside the box'. One director said that "Ted Fort can see things that other people can't". It has been noted that some dyslexics do have this knack and other fellow sufferers have been recognised in this way, such as world famous sailor, Harold Cudmore and Richard Branson. I think it is also one of the reasons for success in my sailing – applying lateral thinking to race tactics. It is not a conscious act: I don't suddenly think, half way up a beat that I need to think outside the box – an alternative direction merely suggests itself. I have the ability to do things differently.

Although Ian could be a little cautious of the big purchase, it has to be said that Fort Vale would not be where it is without his huge talent and dedication. I would not be where I am today without him. His skill in executing commercial activities, building and guiding the team and managing expansion has been paramount. I may have discovered the "oil" but Ian has pumped it.

Ian had been unsure about the purchase of No. 4 Shed and when I decided we needed laser cutting technology, he put his foot down. The laser cutter was, again, something I had seen demonstrated and I was convinced that it was a positive way forward. According to Ian, the sums did not add up. They were extremely expensive, I had to

admit. These Swiss-built machines were around a quarter of a million pounds at a time when the Swiss Franc was strong. But I was convinced and I bought the first machine with my own money rather than with company funds – I was so confident that they would be profitable. It has turned out to be the case. Incidentally, we were fortunate in being able to help the Government at the time of the Gulf War, cutting armour plating for army vehicles. This was a short period when we had to run the machines 24 hours a day, seven days a week to meet demand. This reminded me of the shadow factories of the Second World War, although our contribution was minor in this case.

This was also a period when I was determined that the country should offer industry the best chance to succeed and grow. It was a common concern among like-minded industrialists in the region of north east Lancashire and was identified by local M.P., John Lee, now Lord Lee of Trafford.

John won the election as Conservative candidate for Pendle in May 1979, defeating the Labour candidate, Doug Hoyle. Both now sit in the House of Lords. (An earlier Labour M.P. for Pendle, Sidney Silverman, was famous for pushing through the abolition of capital punishment.) The new M.P. was very active in communicating with industry and instigated the formation of the Pendle Industrialists Club. The Club consisted of many local company owners and managing directors. I supported and was a very active member of the Club. Regular meetings were held to develop strategy. Socially, there was an annual dinner with the likes of Michael Heseltine as speaker. With the contacts that John Lee had in Parliament, the Club became quite a force in lobbying for legislation that would encourage manufacturing

Above: The Pendle Industrialists Club meet Chancellor, Nigel Lawson, at the Houses of Parliament

1   John Ashcroft - Coloroll
2   Jack Gissing - Gissing and Lonsdale (deceased)
3   Peter Lilley MP
4   Ted Fort OBE - Chairman, Fort Vale Engineering Group - Chairman, Pendle Industrialists
5   Kevin Berkins - Fence Gate Inn
6   Ian Wilson - Managing Director, Fort Vale Engineering
7   Derek Evans - Hargreaves, Brown & Benson (died aged 70)
8   Philip Turner - Turner Construction
9   Phillip McIvor - Farmhouse Biscuits
10 Ronnie Foster - Cleveland Guest (deceased)
11 Peter Greenwood - Greenwood Plant Hire and Conservative Association Treasurer (Deceased)
12 John F. Turkington - Turkington Engineering, Burnley
13 John Lee M.P. (at the time; now Lord Lee)
14 The Rt. Hon. Nigel Lawson MP (then Chancellor of the Exchequer - now Lord Lawson)
15 Geoffrey Sutton MBE - Chairman, Weston Engineering (died aged 72)
16 Gina Hearne - Personal Secretary of John Lee MP
17 Alan Taylor - Baxenden Chemicals - Haslingden
18 Tom Clarke - Chairman, Silentnight Group (died aged 73)

industry. Several meetings of the Club with leading politicians, such as Chancellor, Nigel Lawson, influenced the government in many areas such as taxation, training, financial support, export initiatives, etc.

The Club also recognised the importance of training, a fundamental principal of mine, of course, and was a guiding influence of the Pendle Training Group. This body had a training centre in Nelson housing machine tools for hands-on training of apprentices, and others, with supporting theory classes. The training diversified into other industries as demand increased and the centre was an excellent resource, used and supported by local industries.

Over the years, I have met every (Tory) Chancellor, and also the Prime Minister, John Major. In fact, after a meeting with Chancellor George Osborne, in 2014, in his Autumn statement he mentions, "... my friends from Pendle and Burnley...". I like to think that I influenced in a small way his decision to raise capital allowances from £25,000 to £200,000 for small companies.

The company continued to grow and I continued to look for new market areas and opportunities. In the late 1970s, I had heard that the offshore oil industry required a valve for small tanks, which were shipped to the oil rigs with aviation fuel for the servicing of helicopters. These refuelling tanks were manufactured by an existing customer of

Left: M.P. for Pendle, John Lee (now Lord Lee of Trafford), presents to me the BS5750 accreditation certificate at Chatburn in June, 1972. The Pendle Constituency encompasses Nelson and Colne, together with associated smaller districts such as Brierfield, Newchurch, Trawden, Barnoldswick (home of Rolls Royce) etc.

ours and they put me in touch with the operators in Aberdeen. I visited them, detailing our experience, our design skills and explained what would be required in terms of equipment for this duty – manlids, relief valves and discharge valves. This included special valves to check that no water had contaminated the fuel before refuelling an aircraft: very important, of course. My price and the final specification was approved and they placed the order. This, another new design, successful and efficient, aimed at a specific niche market, rolled off the drawing board and into production. The design office must have wondered often what the boss was going to bring back from a trip next time. They never had to wait very long.

One of our competitors was the French company, Gensollen. They too made valves, some of which looked very similar to our own, it has to be said, although the quality was not up to our standards and they were continually lagging behind us in their designs and detailing. Our constant progress in design improvement has long left any competitor in our wake. I heard that Gensollen had been placed in receivership so I set off for Marseille with our French salesman, Jean-Frederic Frot, with the idea of possibly buying the company. I met with their Managing Director and found him to be distraught and almost in tears as he came to terms with the reality of his firm failing. We continued to discuss the possibility of our purchasing the company and he outlined his product range, which included the valves he made for the liquid gas (LPG) industry. He gave me a copy of all the drawings for the LPG valves with which I returned to England. Back at Fort Vale, with the drawings, I went into Dave Smith's office, plopped the drawings on his desk and announced that we were now in the worldwide liquid gas market. Again, this turned out to be a key pivotal moment as we now supply 95 per cent of the world's LPG valves. I didn't buy Gensollen.

But I could always rely on the team to respond to a challenge. They may have grumbled at first when something new came along and I am sure they hated it when I became impatient if a design was not progressing well. I may even have felt the need to raise my voice on occasion: the whole office knew when that happened. The company was working together, systems were in place and Ian was steering the ship, and the crew, in his usual efficient yet friendly manner. This meant that I could continue to steer my sailing ambitions more effectively.

Chapter 12

Racing Ahead

Sailing in the Soling fleet was very competitive, being an Olympic class in those days. The Soling had been chosen as the three-man keelboat class for the Games as it was more economical than others, encouraging amateurs into the class, and it had the desired compromise of performance and seaworthiness, performing well in trials in winds up to 40 knots.

Open meetings and championships necessitated a lot of travelling, often abroad. It was when at one of the Soling events in Denmark that we set on the next overseas Fort Vale distributor in Frank de Fontenay, a native Dane well connected with the transport industry and with a proven sales record. Frank was well respected and liked both by the Fort Vale team and our customers. Economies still had to be made at that time and I remember being very cold sleeping in a tent on that trip. In 1974 I obtained the UK agency for Elvstrom who made and sold Solings and the spares and equipment used on the boats. I had taken to the factory a map of the UK and indicated to the owner, Paul Elvstrom, how we were situated centrally in the country for efficient distribution. Here is another coincidence. Elvstrom is a successful and famous sailor of many years of competition but, as mentioned earlier, his first victory of international standing was in the 1948 Olympic Games. Elvstrom won the gold medal in the Firefly class (the single-handed class in those days) – the class of boat in which I had started racing.

Another trip to Denmark, this time with Graham Murray, turned into a marathon. We had to collect our two new boats. We left Britain on a beautiful spring morning but were somewhat surprised to find icebergs and heavy snow on docking at Esbjerg. In fact it was Europe's worst winter for 30 years and we did not have a warm coat or pair of gloves between us. We left our cars at a hotel and when we awoke in the morning they were nowhere to be seen. The snow was by then eight feet deep and it was to be four hours before diggers could clear enough snow to find our cars. Graham's car engine was never to start again but, fortunately, I had one of the first Range Rover four-wheel-drive cars. We tied Graham's car to the back of the Range Rover and off we went.

At the Soling factory we then had two cars and two rather large keelboats, but with only one car running. We hitched my 27 foot, two

ton boat to the Range Rover then tied Graham's car to the back of my boat trailer and finally hitched Graham's boat on the back of his car. We set off fearlessly, racing across Denmark to catch the ferry with our one hundred foot long boat train. Graham kept on applying the brake but I kept my foot down, not sure if we would reach the port in time. Amazingly we arrived safely at the ferry terminal only to find the engines on the ferry had broken down, so we had a long wait. We did, eventually, arrive back in Britain.

We sailed against each other on Windermere in these two boats for several years and I am happy to record that I managed to beat Graham fairly regularly. We continued to sail together long afterwards, Graham crewing for me in Etchells, Dragons, on larger boats, on the Tofinou and we still share one of the classic 17-foot one-design yachts on Windermere.

After the Munich Olympics in 1972, we had an opportunity to go to Medemblik in Holland for the Soling European Championships. Towing the boat behind a Landrover was a slow process. Held up in a traffic queue, I joked about the damage it would do to the car in front if my foot slipped on the clutch. Needless to say – it did. A cash settlement persuaded the other driver to take matters no further.

On another occasion, in 1976, we were racing in the Soling competing for a place in the British Olympic Team to go to the Montreal Olympics. We motored along with the other members of the British Team across the hills from the previous event at Hyères in

France up to Geneva, where the next event took place. Here most of the Soling crews lived in an underground cavern, which was in fact a modern day fall-out shelter entered through a large steel door in a rock face. It was one of several built in Switzerland in case an atomic bomb was dropped and each would be home for around four hundred people if the need arose. Accommodation was limited to communal bunk bed rooms for up to 30 people, communal showers and kitchens – very cosy, and only £1 a night – we still did things on a shoe-string as far as possible in those days: we had to.

With all the restrictions of Harold Wilson's Labour Government in the Seventies, we were limited to taking abroad a mere £25 in currency. The top rate of income tax rose to 83 per cent and reached 98 per cent when an investment income surcharge was applied. I could, however, sometimes take advantage of the tax reduction applicable when one was abroad for more than 65 days in the year. With overseas exhibitions, visits to customers, sailing events and holidays, I quite often qualified. A good thing about the Wilson years, though, was the one hundred per cent write-down on plant and machinery in the first twelve months.

We had a few days to spare before the Geneva European Championships and there had been a heavy fall of snow on the mountains down to quite a low level. As a result, John Watson, myself and a number of others decided to take off up to Chamonix where, in superb weather, we had three days skiing together in new powder snow. What better combination can there be than good sailing and good skiing? These were great times, but hard work.

I sailed the Soling for many years, firstly with Chris Porritt and Richard Burhouse as crew, then Miles Thompson and David Peach.

With Chris and Miles, I started the next Olympic campaign. We spent many weeks competing in regattas in the UK and Europe, including winter training at Calshot (Southampton). After breaking the ice off the boats we would be craned in by the Fawley power station's huge, 200 tonne crane. In one race I fell in the freezing water but prompt crew action meant that I was quickly retrieved. The top six sailors in the class had to train at Calshot and compete in Weymouth Olympic Week every year: these included Chas Ingham, John Watson, John Oakley, Jamie Clark, Bob Fisher and Barry Dunning, among others in the helmsmen and crew list.

Miles, Chris and I, with my wife, Fay, daughter Jo, and Cathy Thompson (née Darby) had a fantastic holiday at Bermuda Race Week. It was especially memorable as the year was 1979 and the general election voted in Mrs Thatcher. We celebrated with champagne and I know the events following the change of government had a huge impact on the future direction of Fort Vale and the opportunities created.

Below: Sailing my new Soling on Windermere

Miles reminds me of some of the events we attended...
- World Championships in Hanko 1977
- European Championships in La Rochelle 1979
- Bermuda Race Week 1979 (there were $2 to £1)
- National Championships at Holyhead (2nd overall)
- Gourock
- Various WOW weeks (Weymouth Olympic Weeks) and an abortive but very enjoyable 10 days in Hyères.
- We were 2nd in the Class Points Ladder to Phil Crebbin after WOW 1978 – not bad.

My campaign to join the British Olympic Sailing Team was intense. The Soling was the biggest yacht of the six Olympic classes for the 1976 games. The sport was dominated by the South of England until Charles Ingham and I started competing from the Royal Windermere Yacht Club in the North. Chris Porritt, Miles Thompson and I made up the three-man crew in the boat. The National Championships and Olympic qualifiers were held at Weymouth, which was also to become the site for the 2012 Olympic sailing events.

By winning high placings in regattas throughout the country, we were selected to be included in the Olympic squad. As a measure of this standing, we received grant funding to take part in the European Soling Championships, which was fortunate, due to the crippling income taxes that prevailed at the time. As Denis Healey, the Labour Chancellor, said a couple of years before, "the pips will squeak". This extract from a speech given in Lincoln in 1974 was aimed at property speculators but was misreported as "tax the rich until the pips squeak". It was still applicable, however.

Right: Sailing the Soling hard with David Peach and Nigel Harley

*Left: The start of
one of the races in
the Soling World
Championships
in Hanko,
Norway, 1977*

I competed in the qualifying European championships in Medemblik, Holland; Kiel, Germany – (where we stayed in the British Army barracks); Norway (Chris was not present); Hyères in the South of France; Lac Leman, Geneva; La Rochelle in France and Alassio in Italy. The European championships were also held at The Royal Northern YC at Helensburg, Scotland. This wide range of different locations was a great experience in travelling, which was helpful in later business trips.

It was in Norway (and elsewhere) that we came across the 'Super Sailors' of the Eastern Bloc countries. On land, they were kept apart from the other sailors by their 'minders', living in caravans away from the rest of us. On the water, however, without their minders, they would come and chat. These were extremely high-powered yachters and one of note was a Ukranian, Valentin Mankin, a double Olympic gold medallist – winning in the Finn and the Star classes. Cruising about in the start area, he sailed up to us and asked if we could help him with a clue in the Times crossword. He couldn't complete 2-across. He sailed away for a short time before returning to say that it was OK, he had got it now. Not only was he speaking better English than us, he was completing the Times crossword on the water between races.

It was joked that if you were lost in Weymouth you only had to 'ask a Russian' to get back to the sailing club. These sailors were expected to perform. If they weren't in the top echelon in the results, consistently, they would disappear and be replaced in the next event by a new face.

It was at an event at the Royal Southern Yacht Club that I upset a Prime Minister. Getting accommodation at these events could be a problem and we had not been efficient that weekend so arrived with no arrangements in place. There's only one way to tackle this situation. Full of confidence, we walked into an upmarket hotel and announced that we were booked in there and which was our room? Flustered,

Right: I didn't realise I was such a good sailor! An impressive haul of silverware at the Soling British Championships in the 1983 Whyte & Mackay Regatta

the staff checked their bookings and could not find us on the list, of course. We insisted and persevered, eventually being given room number ten, which, having three beds, was the best they could do to accommodate us.

The following morning at breakfast there was a very grumpy Mr. Ted Heath in the dining room. He was down for the start of the Fastnet race. He always stayed at that hotel, we learnt, and he always had room number ten, understandably. He had arrived late, only to find that his room had gone. His room. He had to make do with a most unsatisfactory alternative. I'm afraid we spoilt his stay.

There were usually about 60 boats taking part in our events and we would tend to finish mid-way or late 20's with the odd moments of brilliance. Unfortunately we were not successful at the final Weymouth Olympic trials but were selected as reserves.

Following my various Olympic campaigns in the Soling, in 1985 I progressed to the Etchells class, which is slightly longer at over 30 feet overall. The Soling had ceased to be an Olympic class and although the Etchells is not an Olympic class, it is an excellent boat to sail with good performance and there is a keen fleet, worldwide. It was, in fact, one of the contenders for the Olympic class of keelboat in the trials of 1966/7, which included the Soling. Despite the Etchells emerging clearly as the fastest boat, overall opinion favoured the more affordable Soling.

We sailed with the Clyde fleet to start with at the Royal Gourock Yacht Club. In those days that was the most competitive fleet in the UK, the only other fleet being in Cowes. The Cowes fleet was growing and became larger and more competitive to race in than the Clyde fleet and we took our boat to race at Cowes Week in 1987. I had crewing with me then David Peach and Cameron Still and during that week we won 6 out of the 7 races that we sailed, in spite of having to learn about the extreme tides in the Solent and the complicated courses. This resulted in invitations to The Royal Yacht Squadron for receptions and prize giving. As David Peach and Cameron Still were London based, and as it was as easy for me to get to the Solent as to the Clyde, I then based the Etchells in Cowes and raced from there, as a member of the Royal Corinthian Yacht Club. We continued to compete successfully at Cowes Week for 27 years.

Since that first Cowes Week we have competed overseas in the Etchells many times including World Championships in America (2); in New Zealand (1) and Australia (1); as well as in three UK World Championships regattas. There have been many international regattas, including the Invitational Bermuda Race Week (5); Hong Kong (2); Miami (2) mid-winters and several European regattas in France (12); Monaco (6); Italy (4) and Ireland (1).

I particularly enjoyed Bermuda Race Week. Every first week in May we would compete there, with the Soling in the earlier days and then with the Etchells. Following the Etchells World Championships in San Francisco (1991) and Larchmount (1992), I decided to keep a boat permanently in Bermuda to make sure we received an invitation to Race Week each year.

The Royal Bermuda Yacht Club was extremely male oriented to the point that ladies were not allowed to enter via the main entrance. Prize giving had to be held in the Ladies Annexe in order for them to be able to attend. My wife, Fay, would have none of it and walked through the main entrance defiantly to howls of horror and anger from the male members.

Bermuda was great fun with so much to do to complement the sailing. In my usual manner, I would insist that we made the most of the opportunities and, if we were not on the water, we would be on the greens of the golf course or exploring the island. I got the impression that some of the crew struggled to keep up at times.

Cars were not available for hire in Bermuda so we had to use motor scooters. The use of these came with a certain risk and a comment from a club member alerted us to this – "We don't want any of you visitors sailing here this week to get road rash."

One could, however, use a car if one was available with the house one had rented there. It did entail passing the Bermudan driving test – which was amusing in itself. I did actually pass the test but if an applicant failed the examination, the result was announced to him not in words but in the much more dramatic action of his examination form being torn up in front of him.

Below: Competing in Bermuda Race Week, 1987

But the lifestyle and the 'living life to the full' culture of Bermuda were to catch me out dramatically in subsequent trips there.

As well as sailing in the Etchells, I also enjoyed taking a very active part in the growth and management of the class and served as the Class UK and European President. It was rewarding to encourage others to enter the class and I sponsored a boat in Cowes and another in France.

Sailing in the south of England to such a degree eventually prompted a permanent move to a house on the Beaulieu River. This close proximity to the sailing Mecca of Cowes encouraged further involvement in the Dragon class, which I raced with Graham and Iain and also with our new colleague, James Knight.

James, who works for North Sails, became a regular on board for many of our races and his knowledge of sails and sail setting was immensely helpful.

James also joined us when we sailed in the Sunsail 37s Corporate Fleet in Cowes Week. This larger boat gave me the opportunity to share with some deserving individuals the pleasures to be had from sailing and perhaps to encourage the broadening of their horizons. We would include promising youngsters from Burwain Sailing Club, for instance, who would not normally get the chance to experience Cowes Week.

In 2008 the event had 65 boats entered and included 34 professional skippers, so the competition was keen and the standard of sailing was high. With Graham Murray, Iain Morrison, Sally Armstrong and James Knight as core crew, supported by swop-over guest crew members, I managed to win the event. It was a great achievement and the prize

was a holiday in Greece, not just for one or for a couple but for the entire crew, courtesy of Sunsail.

Another regular regatta we attend is the Royalist Regatta held in Portsmouth each year. The event is organised by the Sea Cadets, an organisation I am pleased to support. The name comes from the Sea Cadets training ship, TS Royalist, their flagship, a 63-feet long brig. Again, larger boats are used such as the Sunsail 37s, and corporate teams from the City are joined by the Royal Navy team, one from Fort Vale and occasionally royalty in the person of the Earl of Wessex.

We need a crew of eight or so on board the boats for the Royalist Regatta. We have a 'core' crew of four seasoned mariners – usually myself, Iain, Graham and James – and we make up the remainder from Fort Vale staff and apprentices. I am delighted to say that all who attend enjoy the sailing, and the social side, and that the sport has been taken up by some of the Fort Vale attendees. 2012 was a particularly memorable year for us at the Royalist Regatta as we managed to win the event by beating our old rivals, the Royal Navy team.

I have to say that I'm becoming a little less athletic and am finding that the Etchells and the Dragon are a little beyond my capabilities these days. I find that my new boat, a Tofinou class, is a lot more sophisticated and the one I now prefer.

The Tofinou is a 9.5 metre long racing dayboat. It has a lifting keel, which makes it much easier to put onto a trailer to be towed on the road. It also has a 15 bhp engine that is very useful for getting out to and returning from the racing area and manoeuvring in marinas.

Right: I'm keeping an eye on the Sunsail winning team, 2008, as they are about to start celebrating our win. Front: Sally Armstrong & Samantha Hartley. Back row from the right: James Knight, apprentice Daniel Wood, John Hartley, Graham Murray, Iain Morrison, with myself holding the silverware

Sailing has been a large part of my life and so very influential. I have been to many interesting and exciting places around the world and made good friends everywhere – many now long-standing. I learnt a great deal from sailing at an international level. It transforms your character, gives you confidence and a broader view of the world.

Faced with a potential strike at Riggs Tools, standing on a workbench and looking down on a sea of workers' faces, I remember thinking, "This is just like the start of a European Championship race. I have to win". And that gave me the confidence to address the meeting.

"Anyone taking an hour off today or leaving the factory before the end of the shift does not have a job – if you go, don't come back tomorrow because I will have closed the factory!"

Below: Sailing my Tofinou in France

I really, really meant it and they realised this from the tone of my voice and my obvious determination: just as determined as on the start line of a race. They all came back to work.

There have been many business links made through contacts on the social side of sailing. New sailing venues have opened up new business opportunities in new locations. Sailing and business: warp and weft.

Sailing was such a key ingredient in my development, particularly as a young man, that I now support and encourage young people to get into the sport and help them to have the opportunity to benefit as I did.

Through the Fort Foundation and the Beaulieu Beaufort Foundation, I like to help young sailors progress with support at events or sponsorship. I take great delight in giving young people the opportunity to get involved in sailing initially, by inviting them to join

Left: The Fort Vale team members of 2010/2011 who sailed in the Royalist Regatta. All started as apprentices with the company. The two on the right took up sailing after the experience and Dave Bailey, second from right, is currently the Technical Director at FV. Graham Blanchard, far right, is Production Manager

our crew at the Royalist Regatta, for example. If I can give them a helping hand in realising their potential through sailing, and in other ways, then I am happy to do so.

It was a great honour to be awarded the Docker Cup by the Royal Thames Yacht Club in recognition of my efforts in promoting sailing to young people. It was also a great surprise when it was announced at the Prizewinner's Dinner, as I'd had no advance notice that I was to receive the Cup. The Docker Cup dates from 1846. It is awarded for "…outstanding services to sailing by any individual…". It is one of the final four very special awards kept secret throughout the proceedings and presented at the end of the evening. To be recognised with such a prestigious award by one's peers is very flattering.

Sailing clubs too sometimes need support and a little help with their infrastructure so that they can offer the facilities to bring on young sailors. I think of my own first sailing club, Burwain, and how helpful and friendly the members there were: a collection of characters all willing to help and encourage. The club now has a junior section and runs structured training courses – wonderful to see. I am still a member there and continue to contribute.

Chapter 13

Flying High

One day in 1991 John Hartley came into my office at Parkfield Works and he began to tell me of a little adventure he'd had at the weekend. Apparently, one of his clients crewed for a hot air balloon team and, as John had expressed an interest, he had been invited to go along to a park in Skipton where the balloon would be taking off very early on the Saturday morning.

He duly arrived at the park and was intrigued as the equipment was assembled and the balloon inflated. As all the preparations were being completed the pilot, Mike Snow, said to John, "Right, get in the basket".

John said that he was not expecting this at all – he'd only gone to watch. He had to make a rapid mental assessment of risk versus adventure but he jumped in and had a wonderful hour's flight over the moors into a quiet valley beyond. The scenery and the experience were breathtaking, he reported. His obvious enthusiasm was infectious. I too am attracted to flight in most of its forms and I wondered if this might be an affordable way to get airborne.

"Shall we get one?" I suggested. "Could we have the name of Fort Vale on the side? Could you see if you can get some ideas and costings together?"

John looked a little taken aback but soon began to realise that perhaps the notion might be possible. He said that Mike Snow had bought his balloon from the manufacturers, Camerons, in Bristol and he would talk the possibilities through with him.

Below: 'Snowman', Mike Snow's balloon

It all came together. As 1992 was the 25th anniversary of the company, I was looking to mark the occasion with something memorable and we had been looking at helicopters: but the service costs would be at least £75,000 a year. A balloon was far more affordable and more visible, too. Later that year we took delivery of a 90,000 cubic feet hot air balloon with Fort Vale livery on the envelope and inflated it at home in Chatburn. Mike Snow was pilot and John's client, Mike Ball, helped with assembly and retrieve. We took off from the paddock alongside my house and floated over the Ribble Valley, over Waddington Fell before landing at some speed and dragging a little over the heather to a stop. What an experience. I realised that this was a great sport and was going to be a lot of fun, not just for me but for friends and colleagues too. It was the opportunity to build an enthusiastic team working together for the benefit of themselves and others.

We decided that the two of us, John and I, would try to qualify as pilots and Mike Snow said that he was prepared to take us on as PUTs (PUT – Pilot Under Training). It can take around a couple of years to qualify, depending on commitment, and written examinations on five subjects as well as practical training to gain one's Pilot's Licence. Unfortunately, although I took several hours training with Mike, I did not have the time to commit to completing the requirements. John did, however, and even though he was still sailing his Solo dinghy on the open meeting circuit, he checked out in 1993.

Several Fort Vale personnel had taken an interest from time to time and John's very first flight after qualifying, and without another pilot on board, was to carry Bill Robinson, Sales Director, for his inaugural experience. "I didn't dare tell Bill until after we landed and were in the pub that I hadn't flown passengers unsupervised before". John said. "Bill took the news very calmly, I have to say."

Another colleague who showed an interest in the balloon was Dave Smith. With his usual level of commitment, he became very involved and took on pilot training himself, under John's tuition.

It was at this time that I had a surprise for John Watson. John and I were having a meeting at Parkfield Works. As well as being a sailing friend in Scotland, he was my stockbroker at Tilney and Co. of Glasgow. I have always continued my interest in stocks and shares ever since that first investment at the age of nineteen.

As it got to five o'clock, I sprang up and said to him, "Right, come on, we're going ballooning".

Left: The first Fort Vale balloon – G-TEDF, here seen ready for take-off from Victory Park, Barnoldswick

Flying High

Right: The replacement balloon, G-FVEL, seen at Simonstone before the Philips glass manufacturing plant was demolished

His face said it all and he was not sure if he could believe me or not. Off we shot, over to Chatburn where Dave and John had the balloon ready, having been briefed by me earlier. Poor old John W was hardly dressed for the occasion in his business suit and smart shoes. We replaced his jacket with a sweater and we all got into the basket. Dave took the controls and we took off. As John W said later, it is a wonderful experience, as the ground seems to drop away from the balloon with no sensation of acceleration or G force.

It was a memorable flight, which culminated in a landing on the top of Hamledon Hill – not the ideal spot but it did have a road leading to the summit where there were a few radio masts. Unfortunately, the gate at the bottom of the road had been fitted with locks and it took the retrieve crew some time to arrange for a key from the Police and get up to us.

Below: In the basket and ready for take-off from the airfield at Chambley

No matter, these things happen and we still managed to get home in time for a glass of bubbly, which is the traditional way to celebrate a first flight, and in time for John to clean his muddy shoes.

The balloon has been a great success in terms of others taking part as well as being an adventure for me. It really is a team activity to get the balloon rigged, in the air and retrieved. The camaraderie following a flight has a real buzz. We have flown hundreds of different people over the years – staff, friends and customers – giving them all the opportunity to experience the delight of floating over the countryside. It is a great pleasure to have enabled this to happen.

I went with the balloon to the huge fiesta held each year at Albuquerque in America. John H and Dave shipped the balloon out to our office in Houston where we inflated it to show customers before

they drove it across to Albuquerque, briefly upsetting a Texas Ranger on the way by driving a little faster than they should. I flew across to meet them there. Nearly one thousand balloons gathered together in an event that brings the city to a halt. It is a magnificent sight and landing on the banks of the Rio Grande is more than a little different in scale to landing on the banks of the Ribble.

At my 65th birthday celebrations at Gleneagles in 2002 I managed to get two of my closest friends into the air. We thought that the weather would beat us but, waking up to a cold and frosty morning, we laid out the balloon on a practice area of the golf course and took off with David Huggins and Iain Morrison on board. It was a classic flight with mist filling the distant valleys and sun glancing the hilltops.

And in Ireland, such a pleasant place to fly: the population is so friendly. It is not uncommon to be invited into a farmhouse after a landing for homemade soda bread and jam with a cup of tea.

In France, I flew at the Chambley fiesta, at an old American airforce base. We helped to set a world record there for the largest number of balloons taking off at the same time. In amongst four hundred or so other balloons, taking off from a long line stretching right down the 2.4 miles-long runway certainly concentrates the mind.

And there is not much to beat the spectacular scenery when flying in the Austrian Alps. I will never forget the last flight I had in Kirchberg when John H popped the balloon down in a tiny field that I was convinced was never big enough to accept us.

The balloon has flown the Fort Vale flag far and wide over more than two decades and is still seen in the skies across the UK and beyond.

Below: Looking down on the Austrian meadows from the balloon basket. The shadow cast by the balloon is visible on the trees, bottom left

Chapter 14

Family and Life

As I said earlier, it was sailing that first brought me together with Fay. I was sailing in the European Championships organised by the Royal Northern Yacht Club – doing quite well, I remember, and finishing second overall.

Fay and I were manoeuvred into adjacent seats at a sailing club dinner by Elizabeth Price. She had been at school in the Lake District with Fay and they had remained good friends. Fay and I got on very well together and conversation flowed. At the end of the meal I asked for her telephone number and, taking out notepad and pen, was ribbed by Chas Ingham, "Another one for your little book, Fort". Chas can be less than diplomatic at times. Fay gave me the number and, there it was again, "Rockcliffe 259". That number, again, 259. Was it an omen? Was this a match made…? It went in the notepad I always carry – the same way that much that occurs in my life does.

I'm not sure if I had become a little more needy following the deaths of my parents. Perhaps the hole it had left needed to be filled.

Right: My bride to be – Fay Paterson

Fay was extremely attractive. As we saw more of each other, the mutual attraction grew and we discovered more about each other too.

Fay lived in Scotland with her young daughter, Joanna, from a previous marriage. When I met her parents, I puzzled over the fact that Fay bore no resemblance to either of them. I could not work it out. However hard I studied her features, there was no commonality at all. Fay was an adopted war baby, it transpired. She had been orphaned and not known her biological parents.

Our relationship was not easy. I was running the business and had a comprehensive sailing programme taking me away to all parts of Europe. There were business trips too. But some of the sailing was in Scotland and we managed to develop the relationship.

We were married in Scotland in September, 1975. It was a traditional church wedding with family and friends. The fact that my parents were gone, as was my previous dependency on them in domestic life, was alluded to by long-time sailing friend, Robin Delves, remarking, "Any port in a storm, Ted". Joke, joke – but probably near to the truth.

In the first year of our marriage I officially adopted Joanna. My solicitors at the time were dead against this but I was committed to the three of us being a family. It appeared to be working although there may have been upsets at times. Fay wrote to me in Kiel when I was sailing there that it had been a "… tremendous year since we met …" and that it had been a "… somewhat stormy passage in the last months but I have no regrets in marrying you". I noted that although she had written the letter on letter headed paper from our house in Read, she was actually back in Scotland. No matter – not odd to be visiting her old home and parents.

Left: Jo and me in the garden at Lancashire Ghyll prior to the move to Read, with Jeeves the dog that decimated Christine Hindle's desk!

The house in Read, the Old Vicarage, was bought by myself on the sale of Lancashire Ghyll. Brother Robert had already moved to Higher Hague Farm. I was away when we moved house. I had travelled to Denmark to collect the new Soling but before I left, I told Fay that I wanted a controlled move out from Lancashire Ghyll which was, after all, the family home where I had so many memories. When I got back, the move was already completed, very suddenly and with a clean break. There were Fay and Joanna firmly ensconced in the new home and all connections severed with Lancashire Ghyll. I was never to return to the old farmhouse – it was most sad. I guess that Fay was wanting to make that break a clean one and start her new life without debris from the past but I still feel sad about the suddenness of the departure from twenty eight years-worth of roots.

The Old Vicarage was large enough for our small family at the time – and Jeeves, the dog. Fay enjoyed gardening and was skilled with the flower beds, creating splendid, colourful displays – much as my mother had done at Lancashire Ghyll. Of course, Fay was proud of her new abode and, quite rightly, was anxious to invite her parents down to visit.

It was at the time of one of her parents' visits that, on returning home after a hard days work, there was nothing for me to eat. This was not normal for me and was more than a little disappointing: I'm afraid I threw a bit of a wobbler. I had been through a shattering few weeks at the factory. I was tired and hungry and was being told, in my own home, where I should have been supported and comforted to my mind, that dinner was not for another hour and a half whatever my demands. I was of the way of life that when the worker came home from the mill, he was fed. I took my hunger, hurt and anger to the pub where good food and much ale went someway to comforting me. On returning home, I knocked all the sailing trophies off a shelf on my way upstairs to bed, making a tremendous clatter but was past caring. It was remarked upon in derogatory terms next morning.

I hoped that Fay would join me in my world more fully. Would she take to the 'warp and weft' of sailing, business, engineering and travel that made up my existence? She was not a great sailor and not very interested in the business initially. She did pop in to Parkfield Works on occasion. I remember that she once wrote to me when I was away saying that she had visited the works and that "…everyone seemed to be working hard" – which, I feel, was what she thought a boss might want to hear or have reported back to him.

Above: posing for a photograph with Fay and Jo on the Soling at Windermere

Fay and Joanna did join me in Italy, at the 1975 Soling European Championships at Alassio. I was sailing the boat that I had named 'Romance' following our own. She loved Bermuda, of course, and the Isle of Wight where she came with me when I was sailing Allan Bulmer's yacht at Cowes in 1983.

Fay did make a huge effort with considerable sacrifice when joining me on business trips. In the early days of seeking out export markets, money was still scarce and trips to some of the more expensive countries had to be made on a tight budget. The Scandinavian countries were particularly pricey so, on a business trip to Sweden, Fay and I camped. I had done this before but not with Fay. It must have seemed most bizarre to see an English businessman emerging from a small tent in the morning dressed in a suit and carrying a brief case, like something

Left: Fay and me manning the stand at the Offshore Exhibition in Singapore, 1984

Above: The village of Chatburn beneath the moody slopes of Pendle Hill, near Clitheroe

from Monty Python. I bought a camping stove for the trip and claimed it as a business expense. The VAT man was not for accepting it but I won the argument after explaining that it was all to save money by camping rather than staying in an expensive hotel. Perhaps I should suggest this cost-saving strategy to the current sales staff?

We undertook expeditions such as an Engineering Industries Association four-week mission to Australia and New Zealand when she was one of only two ladies in a party of dozens of businessmen. Together we manned a Fort Vale company stand at various exhibitions, including one in Singapore. Fay was always the perfect partner at business functions and awards. A visit to Australia was a particularly important one at the time. We were trying to increase our presence in the transport industry there. There were some on the trip who combined it with a little extra-marital activity. One day the organiser of the trip intercepted a certain party in the lift with the girlfriend – not in a compromising situation, I can add, but to whisper in his ear that his wife had arrived and was on the way up to see him.

On 18th January, 1979, which was Fay's birthday, we moved to a new home, a very splendid house in the village of Chatburn, under the flanks of Pendle Hill – a hill of many moods but always impressive. I have to say that I was a bit of a bystander in the operation of moving in. It all seemed to happen without my input. Fay was in control and it was almost a case of coming home from a trip away one day to a different address and that was that. The Old Vicarage had been cleared and we were established at Chatburn. You may pick up from my narrative that I was none too comfortable with this situation. I was not at the centre of operations as I would more normally be.

The house and grounds were tremendous, though. Fay did get engrossed in developing the garden, which we planned together. We added outbuildings, new beds, a tennis court and planted trees. I take great pleasure in planting trees.

Trees are there far longer than the man who plants them – hopefully. They are a legacy that one can leave. I have a strong desire, a need to leave my own legacy: trees are a part of it; this book is too. I've always planted trees at all my properties – right from the early days at Lancashire Ghyll.

With a similar intention, I began my stone folly building with arches and walls from reclaimed Lancashire stone. It reflects the local character and reminds me of the industrial past of the area, which is so important to me. We obtained and added adjacent land when it became available, bringing the total area of land to 48 acres over time. Fay had always liked horses and so Joanna had grown up with them. We built a stable block, which had also two double garages and a tall boathouse section to take a Soling on trailer with sail loft above. We had four horses at one stage. Fay wanted yet another one but I had had enough, she was getting carried away. "The rule is," I told her, "one in – one out". It had the desired effect.

Most of my sailing at this time was at the Royal Gourock Yacht Club on the Clyde so we decided to have a Scottish base. We both loved Fay's parents' village of Rockliffe, on the north shore of the Solway Firth. A splendid property, Castle Hill, became available and we snapped it up. The views from the house were magnificent.

Sailing and business trips kept me on the move a lot of the time but we managed holidays together when we could. A trip to Montserrat

Above: A very proud father with Philippa

was so enjoyable – exploring the island and flying over the volcano – that we decided to purchase a holiday retreat there. In 1984 we bought 'The Lookout', a bungalow perched higher on the island than most with a pool, superb views and a long path down to a beach – perfect.

On another occasion we went on a walking holiday in New Zealand. We had four days walking and three nights following the track of the early explorer, McKinnon, who first blazed a trail from Queenstown to Milford Sound in 1888. I thought it was my best trip ever. Fay hated it. We stayed each night in track lodges. They were very basic and the men slept in one bunkhouse, the ladies in another. Fay hated having to share and sleep in the company of other ladies. I thought the holiday was the greatest adventure of my life.

We decided on India for one holiday but it was not the exotic break we had hoped for. Fay was bitten by a monkey. We rang for a doctor since Fay obviously required a rabies injection as a precaution following the bite. He called in at our hotel room but, as is the case in India, he wanted cash up front – and a substantial amount was involved. Not being used to this procedure I put on my business hat and began to try to negotiate. The doctor was shocked – this was not the response he expected. He remonstrated that Fay needed sympathy, not a discussion on price. Fortunately, I always carry a sufficient amount in cash now to cover possible unexpected situations. The incident spoiled the holiday: it took the shine and shimmer away from what could have been glorious. Fay suffered food poisoning on top of having been bitten and undergoing the unpleasant rabies injection. She felt very unwell when we returned to England.

The doctor in Clitheroe was consulted as Fay continued to be unwell. We wanted his opinion on what we suspected might be dysentery. Fay had gone along on her own to the Health Centre hoping for a solution to her discomfort. The doctor examined her. "You do realise you are pregnant, Mrs. Fort?" he said, at which point Fay fainted. She was not at all well and this last shock was too much.

The obstetrician expressed concern that the foetus may have been damaged due to the possible combined effects of the monkey bite, rabies injection and food poisoning. To our great consternation, he thought that there might be the slight chance that the damage could be serious enough to consider an abortion and that Fay should have a scan immediately to check that all was well. The scan was carried out and, to the immense relief of us both, everything was in order and the foetus was healthy.

We were absolutely thrilled and delighted when Philippa was born wholly well after her ordeal. It was a joy for us all.

So at the age of twenty, Joanna had a little sister.

It was two years later that I was sailing at Bermuda Race Week again, having been invited there as a previous Olympic team member. Each year I really looked forward to this event and had gone this time with the crew but without Fay – and I went off the rails.

We were young – well, young enough – to behave in a boisterous manner; we had money the weather, the atmosphere and the fitness. Bermuda at that time, in some circles, had a culture of drinking and bed-hopping. The crew were staying with a lady called Alison – very attractive, very attentive. Later I saw the registration number on her car – B 259. That number – was it to be – again?

Alison was somewhat older than me – by some nine years, it transpired. She was older by the same number of years as Kathleen Bedford. She didn't look it – not one bit. We were there at dinner and she stroked the back of my hand. "You are very special," she said, "I like you very much". She made me feel cared for and appreciated. She was the catalyst, the reaction was started and it was explosive. The years of frustration, the pent up desires were released "…like a coiled spring," she said.

She wasn't a gold digger, I knew. She was wealthy in her own right and married to a successful entrepreneur with a large business empire and, allegedly, a lively lifestyle. Alison had seen the world and had experience of wealth on a higher plane than mine. She was encouraging and gave me confidence by saying "You are very smug, you know. You could do more, you could do better in life". I took that on board: it was not quite one of my 'pivotal moments' but it was an influence, definitely. It changed my approach to things.

We saw each other from time to time, in Bermuda and back in the UK, over the next six months. It was clear that Alison did not see me merely as a Bermudan fly-by-night but had genuine affection for me – as I did for her. But it was only for the six months as it turned out.

Foolishly, I had left Alison's telephone number in my wallet. Fay had got my wallet for some reason and found the number – she rang it. The game was up. The next conversation was with a solicitor representing Fay and demanding recompense or divorce. Why the choice, I wondered? Why "OR divorce"? Either it was a serious enough crime for divorce or it was not – but blackmail?

It was clear, however, that the liaison with Alison had to be terminated. I rang and explained. "Oh, Ted," she said, "how sad, the light has gone out".

The divorce proceedings and settlement took two years to conclude: the 'clean break' was achieved finally in 1991, although I have continued to support Fay financially in many additional ways over the years.

We were in Chatburn in 1978; Philippa was born in 1987 and we parted in 1989 when Philippa was just two years old. I only saw

Philippa on rare occasions after that. She was with her mother, of course, back in Scotland at their house (following the settlement), Castle Hill. There was little chance to bond and I believe that the inevitable animosity felt by her mother must have influenced Pippa. Aren't children always the unfortunate casualties? I still can't get through to Pippa, although I'd like to so much. We have missed out on a tremendous amount. I know I am the cause of distress but it has been over 25 years now and I am always hopeful of reconciliation. It's not as though she has been abandoned financially either, far from it – although that is of a secondary consideration to me when compared to family and emotions. Her lifestyle has been supported and her personal wealth assured: but as I say, I still hope for a meaningful relationship.

With Jo it was different. In the early years we had time together where we could communicate, one-to-one, not possible with Pippa, and it made all the difference. Jo could form her own opinions to balance those of her mother. There have been difficult times – aren't there always when dealing with me, whoever you are – but we have always managed to talk. It is a pleasure to see her ambitious and successful in her livery business and settled with husband and two children – my grandchildren. I am pleased, also, that I have been able to help financially in her plans. I love to give ambition and enthusiasm a helping hand where there is potential.

So I had a divorced ex-wife in Scotland with daughters Pippa and Jo. I was left in Chatburn on my own. I was not to know it at the time but this was the beginning of a period of time without much family contact at all. There was the occasional visit to or from Pippa or Jo but not much more. Any other contact tended to centre around affairs that needed to be addressed or financial support of some kind.

There was plenty going on at work to keep me occupied, of course, and the energetic pace of business also may have played a part in aggravating the family situation in addition to my indiscretions. Although the latter was the obvious trigger of events, it cannot have been a very companionable life for Fay prior to the split – not one in which she can have felt comfortable and satisfied, I feel, with all my trips abroad and sailing commitments as well.

It was a period of rapid expansion, of acquisitions, of establishing overseas operations, of developing markets – and of successes.

My sailing programme was as busy as ever, taking me 'hither and yon' across the globe. I had moved from the Soling class to sailing Etchells – another very competitive international fleet.

There were other matters to deal with, too. The house in Montserrat had scarcely been used by us but it was still a huge shock when, in 1995, the previously inert volcano on the Soufrière Hills suddenly and unexpectedly erupted. The small island, only the size of the Isle of

Man, measuring 10 miles by 7, was devastated with the capital town, Plymouth, being totally destroyed. A huge area of the island, over half of the total, was made into an exclusion zone due to the potential danger of pyrocalstic flow and this remains today. Two thirds of the island's population was forced to evacuate. Only around 6,000 now live there from a previous population of 13,000. The volcano remained sporadically active until 2010 and is still monitored.

This was a particularly cruel blow to the island, which had already suffered severe damage when hurricane Hugo struck in 1989. Winds of up to 87 m.p.h. caused severe damage including the closure of the AIR recording studio. The studio, run by Sir George Martin, had many famous bands record there over the years. They included The Beatles, Dire Straits, The Police, Sir Paul McCartney, Sir Elton John, Duran Duran, Michael Jackson, Stevie Wonder, Ultravox, The Rolling Stones, Lou Reed, Black Sabbath and Eric Clapton.

When I bought the Lookout, I was told that some damage to a lino floor in the house had been caused by a visiting Ringo Star who got carried away with some energetic dancing – in his golf shoes!

By sheer chance, our house was in the northwest part of the island and had been spared any damage from the volcano. The hurricane had caused some breakages earlier but nothing too major. The property was repaired and rented out for many years. At times it was occupied by scientists studying the volcano.

I did not return but, much later, Fay took up residence there to take advantage of the location and the most pleasant climate. The girls had left home by then.

Now on my own, in Lancashire, I could knuckle down to developing the business and the creation of some more in the way of wealth – why wouldn't I? Warp and weft.

Chapter 15

Expanding to Succeed

I have always said that with wealth comes responsibility. It is the wealth that I help to create that contributes to society – to running life. When I was forty, I realised that my job was to create wealth. There has to be a wealth creating section of society to keep things ticking: ultimately, wealth runs the local services – fire station, ambulances, the social services, schools, etc. It keeps people in work, feeds families, buys houses, and creates 'disposable income'. That was my job – to create the wealth. To create wealth, one has to succeed.

I did not think of 'success' in terms of static targets but more of 'successful evolution' – one level leading to the next in a natural progression. Others, however, did recognise particular levels of achievement, symbolic points in time. It was always very rewarding to be recognised with an award and it made me proud of our achievements – proud of the entire team, from the apprentices to the designers; the machine operators to the directors. Awards are always a point of reflection for me. They signal times to ponder on our humble beginnings and on how well we have progressed. I never forget my origins – neither my business beginnings nor my personal roots – they were so instrumental in forming the character of the person and of the company.

Success was rewarded in 1981 with our first Queen's Award for Export Achievement. The superb performance of the sales team, headed by Sales Director, Bernard Ineson, supported by Ian Wilson, the design office and the production team had resulted in phenomenal

Right: I hold the Queen's Award, standing next to the Lord Lieutenant of Lancashire, at the presentation on the shop floor at Parkfield Works in 1981, which was in addition to the Buckingham Palace presentation

export figures. Our travels abroad to visit customers, to show our designs at the many overseas exhibitions and our involvement in the evolution of the industry had paid off. Exporting was and still is the major part of our production with over 90% of our output going abroad. The company has been awarded with two Queen's Awards for Export Achievement and a further two for the later Queen's Award for International Trading – the more recent title.

The elation of receiving the award was followed swiftly by the realisation that I had to go to meet the Queen. The thought made me extremely anxious. Although an ardent supporter of the monarchy, to go to Buckingham Palace and to actually meet Her Majesty to receive the award was a daunting prospect.

A party of three was assembled for the trip to London. Brother Robert had to go – I insisted. In spite of his loathing of ceremony, he had to realise that he was a major player in the success of the company, and be recognised for it. Ian Wilson was the third man. He had raised the organisational and professional standards in our commercial operations to a level of performance resulting in this achievement.

Buckingham Palace never fails to impress. I have been invited there for functions several times now but that very first visit was the greatest for awe and wonder. From the collections of fine art on the walls to the height of the massive double doors or the intricate decoration of the plaster work, the scale of every element was almost overwhelming. The combination of these visual aspects and the pomp and ceremony of the whole procedure had a humbling effect and did nothing to calm my nerves.

My turn came as the double doors swung open and my name was called – or bellowed, more like, in a voice that commanded instant reaction. I complied and advanced.

The Queen is small in stature, which I knew, but it was still a surprise to see her so. I approached, turned to face Her Majesty and, after an attempt at a formal bow, advanced my trembling hand to take the one that she offered. I mumbled something by way of an apology for my tremblings. Silently, smiling, she took my hand and laid her other upon it so as to steady my physical jitters but which also calmed me inside. The Queen came across in an instant as an understanding, caring lady in total command of a situation – without saying a word.

It was an amazing experience that I will never forget. On leaving the Palace and still on somewhat of a high, we "three Musketeers" decided to make the most of our visit to the capital. Commandeering a taxi and the driver's local knowledge, we started a tour of some of the nightclubs in the big city. We visited several, I seem to remember, before ending up in Peter Stringfellows, where we enjoyed the scenery for some time. Leaving at three in the morning and hailing a taxi once more, we were flabbergasted to discover the driver was the very same one who had started us out on our nocturnal adventures.

The drive to conquer more overseas markets demanded further commitment and I established our American office and distribution centre in Houston, Texas, a year later, in 1982. Margaret Thatcher was Prime Minister. It was our first base overseas and laid the foundation for global expansion: it was an enormous step forward. The founding of Fort Vale Incorporated has a story behind it too. Bernard Ineson and I went to an exhibition in Bahrain. The exhibition was very different to those we were used to attending. It certainly felt strange to Bernard and me, talking to Arabs wearing headgear and sandals, we in our business suits, explaining to them what our products were used for. The upshot was that we did not get any orders all week. I said to Bernard that we must try to do something more proactive.

I had met a businessman called Harry West from Houston who I had tried to get to help us out in the States. He was very, very reluctant to take on the Fort Vale Agency for spares for relief valves but I managed to persuade him to open a depot in Houston so that we could ensure the Sea Containers' tanks were serviced and repaired by Fort Vale. I felt this to be very important in establishing a reliable US service for our American customers. A national service company always had the advantage over one based overseas.

It is another crucial set of coincidences and a pivotal moment that Fort Vale Inc. began by my meeting Harry West at an exhibition in Bahrain and my persuading him to look seriously at starting the company. It may have been a bit of a rocky start but the company has been operating successfully for over thirty years.

Below: 1987 and I visit Buckingham Palace again – to collect my OBE this time

The Fort Vale Inc. office was established in spite of all. I had eventually to sack Harry West for doubling the value of our products and taking a cut himself. He was replaced by Jim Manke, who used to work for him, and Jim really started to get the operation functioning efficiently. Tragically, Jim later died, far too young, in a tractor accident.

It was in the following year, 1987, that I returned to the Palace. Another surprise – I was honoured with an OBE.

I had been away on business for two weeks and returned home to Chatburn rather tired. "Anything important in the post, Darling?" I asked, not really wanting to tackle the pile of waiting letters.

"No – nothing at all," replied Fay.

It was some time later, flicking through the post, that a particular envelope caught my eye. It was marked, "Urgent – from the office of the Prime Minister".

Hang on – nothing important: she had to be kidding. The letter stated that I had been awarded the OBE. The citation read, "For service to industry". I was taken aback, I have to say, but very proud to receive such recognition. I knew we were progressing well as a company but I had not realised just how well. This acknowledgement of achievement, following closely behind another Queen's Award, confirmed the fact that I really was performing well in engineering and in business.

To put it in context, it was the period when I had bought No. 4 Shed of Valley Mills, I had changed my class of boat from Solings to Etchells, I had won the first Cowes regatta in the boat, I was travelling around the world constantly, for business or sailing – and popping to the Palace for the occasional award. Customers had to be visited, new product designs developed, tests and certifications organised, and new machines purchased.

I was also managing an increasing personal wealth. It had reached the level, for instance, where I could buy the latest Swiss laser cutting machine personally. An increasing amount of time was needed to monitor and trade in my investments on the stock market.

It all added up to a very busy life. I did have excellent help in many areas, of course it was vital, but it all had to be controlled overall and key decisions made at many stages.

I had already established a design and print company with John Hartley as partner. As well as being a long-term sailing friend, John has always been around at Fort Vale. In the early days at Norfolk Street, he worked for me in his school holidays and, of course, he crewed for me in our epic Firefly Championships in Ireland among others. John reminds me of the intensity of our efforts at Norfolk Street – "I always remember that you were a hard taskmaster," he recalls. "I must have been about seventeen years old. When I was working on the Dufil machines, threading 10259 adapters, you would ask how many I'd produced in the last hour. I may have replied, say, that I'd finished 44. 'What?' you would exclaim, with feeling, 'You should be doing at least 50!'"

Oh dear. Yes it was intense – every operation was timed to the minute and parts costed to the halfpenny. John was not put off by my rantings, remarkably. In the preparation of our move to Parkfield Works I had him assembling shelving in the stores area. When at the University of Leeds and at the Royal College of Art gaining a second degree, he would help Bernard Ineson in the preparation of exhibitions and sales literature in his vacation periods. He worked in the drawing office (I delight in reminding him of the dipstick carrier for AD tankers he designed). John created the Fort Vale corporate identity, which gave the company a truly professional and upmarket image and which has stood the test of time well. He, like myself, is still a member of Burwain Sailing Club and we, with Robin Delves, must now be among the longest subscribing members there.

The identification of the tank container market as one with huge potential was proving to be crucial. That memo I had sent round to staff in 1977 to focus our efforts had turned out to be another key and pivotal moment defining our expansion and global reach. Our continuing push into exports was expanded with the establishment of our Dutch company in Rotterdam, Fort Vale BV Rotterdam, in 1989. Like Houston, Rotterdam was another major hub for the transportation of containers, including our own interest, the tank container. Depots for storage, cleaning and refurbishment of tanks were centred on these hubs and they needed valves and equipment on hand, supplied promptly.

The manufacture of tank containers has moved around the globe too. Our first contact as suppliers to the manufacturers was in Ireland with CPV. Tanks were also made in the UK and Europe, principally at manufacturers of road tankers who used their skills in the new and ever-expanding international tank container market.

As the worldwide demand increased, the numbers of units manufactured increased to a point where economies of scale were vital to gain orders against competitors. Production moved to more specialist plants in areas of cheaper overheads and labour. There were casualties. The French company, Hugonnet, succumbed to the pressure of decreasing prices and brought in the receivers. They owed us a lot of money: it was an extremely serious situation. I chartered a plane and we flew over to Dijon in an attempt at recovering some of the debt. (It's odd what we remember from the past but I distinctly recall the pilot asking us all if we had visited the loo as there was no toilet on board the small charter aircraft.)

The Receiver was very polite and explained the situation in detail but there was to be no recompense. We had no insurance against bad

Right: Fort Vale B.V. in Ridderkerk, near Rotterdam, the Netherlands

debts at that time. The loss was very nearly fatal. If someone were to ask me now whether to take out insurance against fire or bad debts, I would always recommend the latter. I certainly make sure we are always covered for unpaid amounts.

South Africa became a centre for a good period and we set up a sales company there, Fort Vale Pty. in 1997. The South African tank manufacturing company, Consani, was another bad debtor for us, I'm afraid. Apparently, the industry already knew them as '...muggers and robbers...' I learnt, but too late. The South African concentration of manufacturing continued for several years and I was keen to set up a production centre there to aid supply. The distance from the UK added weeks to a delivery schedule. It seemed to me that if we did not improve our response times then a competitor could well jump in first and steal the march. Ian and I visited the country several times and had this thought in mind. We were continually assessing the possibilities as we travelled around visiting customers.

But, as Ian Wilson often reminds me, "There is nothing more permanent than change". Ian had never been impressed with the culture and work ethic in South Africa. He thought that setting up a factory there would be a mistake. At the same time the winds of change were felt once more. The Chinese industrialists were investigating the industry and sniffing around. One UK tank manufacturer had already negotiated an arrangement with a Chinese builder and had actually brought a visiting delegation to inspect Fort Vale and check the quality of our equipment that was being fitted to their tanks. The writing was on the wall. Ian identified the turning tide and persuaded me that South Africa would be an error.

The dwindling of the South African market coincided with a tragedy, felt by all of us, when our friend and colleague, the man running our operation on the ground there, Gianni Testa, was killed in a road traffic accident whilst returning from a business trip.

China took the lead in the manufacture of the bulk production of standard tank containers and Ian established an office there in 2002. The more niche-market tank types required in much smaller numbers were still made at specialist manufacturers, such as Universal Bulk Handling in Burscough Bridge or M1 Engineering in Bradford. Niche tanks included liquid gas tanks and offshore helicopter refuelling tanks – both fitted with Fort Vale products.

I was also on the lookout for other companies to acquire. We had set up Sparta Metals based in No. 4 Shed to promote sub-contract laser cutting and other engineering manufacturing services. Sparta was home-grown, as opposed to an acquisition but it started me thinking in terms of diversification. I concluded that, if a company could be

*Right: Francis
searchlights sweep
the skies over Paris
from the Eiffel Tower
in a computerised
display of moving
beams of light*

*Far right: The
Makkah Clock
Tower in Saudi
Arabia with
Francis searchlights
throwing powerful
rays into the sky*

Right: Francis searchlights sweep the skies over Paris from the Eiffel Tower in a computerised display of moving beams of light

Far right: The Makkah Clock Tower in Saudi Arabia with Francis searchlights throwing powerful rays into the sky

acquired at a reasonable cost and had an engineering base – one that I would understand – then it should be considered.

I visited several potential companies that had fallen on hard times. Some were hopeless cases and I walked away very quickly. The one that really caught my interest was Francis Searchlights in Bolton. This was a company established in 1904 with a long history of supplying searchlights to the Royal Navy and throughout both World Wars, as well as to merchant ships and land-based installations. The range of products was produced in-house and to a high standard. I could see potential for product development and a good existing customer base.

The details were finalised and I took over the company in 1990. I kept on the existing staff – their experience and in-depth knowledge of both the market and the product was invaluable. A little administrative reorganisation soon had things ship-shape again. There were some traditional practices which were unacceptable and one of these – the manipulation of performance figures to artificially boost bonus levels – was totally out of order and I did, I'm afraid, demand the removal of the head man there at the time.

I had to put in our own man, Malcolm Dobson, who has managed the company very successfully ever since. The great thing is that Malcolm joined Fort Vale as a young man and progressed his career within the company to reach the high level needed to take charge of Francis.

I am proud to report that the searchlights describing impressive arcs of light over Paris from the top of the Eiffel Tower are ours.

Left: Marine searchlights produced by Francis Searchlights

Below: Francis have been supplying signalling lamps and searchlights to the Royal Navy for decades

There are four Francis 'Moonraker' searchlights on the tower in total. The Makkah Clock Tower in Saudi Arabia is the tallest clock tower in the world at 601 metres high and it is the third tallest building in the world. The tower houses an impressive installation of some forty Francis searchlights with computer controlled roving beams and static lights. There are others nearer home, such as at Blackpool Pleasure Beach and Arsenal Football Club.

At about the same time as Francis, we took on board a company based in Malvern and moved them to premises in Nelson. Autopack make high quality, stainless steel machines and equipment for the dispensing of pie fillings and the like in the food production industry. I combined them with our long-established company, Rigg Brothers Tools to form Riggs Autopack. The commercial and technological support the company can rely on as part of the Fort Vale Group of companies has given Riggs Autopack the confidence to progress and

Below: The Francis Searchlights 'Voyager 2' Searchlight, designed for superyachts

thrive. They continue to be highly successful in their market under the guidance of Nigel Matthews, whom I met originally in the stores of Autopack in Malvern.

When in discussions with the Receiver there, I asked to talk to one of the staff. As I have mentioned previously, I always manage to get a truer picture of affairs from the shop floor. Nigel was Works Manager, having been at the company for twelve years since being an apprentice – a good reference immediately, in my book. But the company had gone into receivership and I was trying to get to the bottom of things. "You can't be very good at your job," was my deliberately aggressive initial comment, "You have one million pounds-worth of stock and you still can't meet your orders". It had the desired affect and Nigel went on the defensive.

"Let me show you this stock" he said and led me to the stores department. "Here is the one million pounds-worth on the books," he said, showing me racks of dust-covered, ancient components. "There is only ten per cent of this lot I can use. It's all out of date".

I wrote in my notepad – "Stock only worth 10% of valuation". It was the desired piece of information and instrumental in revaluing the company more realistically, resulting in the acquisition.

I bought the company for £50,000 and the owner, who had gone bankrupt, said to me, "Well, you might be a successful business man and be buying my business but at least I don't have your grey hair".

Another company to join us at Riggs Autopack was J.B.Hyde, manufacturers of machines for braiding rope. The market was a diminishing one for this product and was reduced, finally, to sales

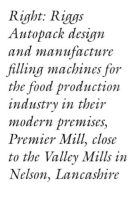

Right: Riggs Autopack design and manufacture filling machines for the food production industry in their modern premises, Premier Mill, close to the Valley Mills in Nelson, Lancashire

of a few spare parts for existing machines and the operation died a natural death.

Betabite was another engineering company managed by Malcolm Dobson. They made hydraulic pipe fittings and supplied manufacturers of agricultural and other vehicles, underground train rolling stock and many other areas. The use of hydraulics in industry is widespread and the quantity of component parts required is huge. Because of this, the market is very competitive and far-eastern manufacturing bases produced cheaper products. Although the Betabite range was extensive and stocks were close to end-users, I could see the writing on the wall and we disposed of the business in 2014. It failed, finally, in 2015.

So not all of the businesses have been long-term successes although they have all played their part to some degree. They have all been associated with engineering in the main. A good example of the consequential results of my looking at businesses for acquiring was the way I started production of metal castings in our own foundry.

For years, we had bought in castings that went into the production of the valves made at Fort Vale. I had already been advised that it was a bad idea to consider in-house casting by the man in charge of the National Engineering Laboratory in East Kilbride in Scotland, who had said, "You want to set up a foundry? You're crazy".

A foundry we knew of was in trouble. Midland Investment Casting was going bankrupt. The owner came to see me at Parkfield Works to discuss my buying the business. I had seen the figures and had a good idea of a fair and reasonable price for the business to make it worth the investment. I said to the owner that he had one chance to name his price – one chance and I would give him a yes or no answer. He did and I said, "No". It is most unfortunate that just two weeks later the pressure on the owner through his business problems proved too much and he committed suicide.

I did buy the company and we continued to serve their existing customers as well as producing castings for Fort Vale. Times were

Above: Casting stainless steel at the foundry in Nelson

still hard in the casting industry. The day the minimum wage was introduced, I had to let several women in the wax department go. The extra costs just tipped the balance – it was unavoidable. The girls cried as they left – it was a close-knit group in the wax room.

Ian Wilson thought we should move all casting requirements for the Group down to the midlands, to Kidderminster where the foundry was located. Frank Hall did not agree and I, too, felt that we would be better served with a local facility: I could see the bigger picture. I decided to set up a foundry in Nelson. The key man at the foundry, the hands-on man who made things tick was John Corrigan. Taking John on board in Nelson, we started casting stainless steel in our own foundry that we established in No. 4 Shed, Valley Mills and by a new company, Fort Vale Castings Limited. With our in-house metal processing we could also recycle more of our production scrap metal. The foundry has been a great success and was expanded in 1999 with a purpose-built facility on the site of what had been No.2 Shed, Valley Mills.

Another coincidence helped here, once again. A foundry in Bradford had failed and I bought the business. Frank Hall was able to strip out all the equipment there, transport it across and install it in the new foundry building. So South Valley Foundry was up and running well very quickly.

I have had my disappointments in business as well. It usually comes down to people or, should I say, a person. Sometimes I can be too trustworthy of individuals too soon and forget my own saying, "Money-power corrupts". Occasionally it happens that when a person gains sufficient control over the financial side of an operation, personal wealth becomes the main objective to such an extent that they lose sight of their responsibilities – and reason. Ambition turns to greed and, sometimes, to such an extent that it reaches dishonesty or even criminality.

It can become so entrenched a practice in an operation that a person may convince himself in time that a malpractice is the norm, and acceptable (as at Francis Searchlights). They can get to a point where they commit ludicrous actions but are somehow blind to reality. For example, one manager was fiddling his monthly bonus, which depended on output. He ran a small offshoot company, Marathon Engineering, which I had set up in the original Norfolk Street premises. He would hide suppliers' invoices in a drawer to boost profit figures. One month he was a little light on output but delivered a box of machine parts to a customer with an invoice, hoping to come away with a cheque. The box went into the customer's stores, which was quite usual and such a box might stay on the shelf, in stock, for some time before being needed. This one was needed immediately, however, and the box was

Left: The manufacturing centre in China – Fort Vale Shanghai Limited

opened only to discover a pile of bricks. That is how ludicrous things can get as corruption takes hold of the mind.

There have been one or two other instances, more usually in areas other than engineering. I was persuaded to be involved in an internet business at one time. The man in charge was a retired bank manager, my financial secretary and respected. When I wanted to dispose of the business, I expected him to vote in favour of the motion with his small share holdings but he sided with the opposition, the management of the company, causing all sorts of problems before we could sort it all out. This betrayal of my trust was very disappointing.

An estate manager at my house in the south of England thought he might get away with rerouting parts of orders for my home and gardens to his house in France. It beggars belief that perpetrators can think that they will get away with such crazy behaviour. "Money-power corrupts" – not with everyone, of course, but be aware.

Another emerging market for Fort Vale products was Russia. With the more open trading arrangements, which had become possible after 1989 with Russia, their requirements for valves for tank containers had grown, particularly in the transporting of liquid petroleum gas. I had visited Moscow and decided that we needed a base there. Our Moscow office was set up in 1995.

The emergence of what we now term the Global Market brought on many changes. The growth of the manufacture of tank containers in China reached such a level that it became inevitable that Fort Vale would have to start manufacturing there. After Ian had set up our Chinese office in 2002, Fort Vale Shanghai Limited, he followed this with a manufacturing centre there in 2005. The same arguments that applied to supplying South Africa applied here – deliveries would take too long from the UK. Manufacturing was limited to simpler

Below: Fort Vale Pte Limited, Singapore

production for a time as the plant grew in capability. Local supply of large batch production close to the market centre was essential to the supply chain. Economics played a part, of course, and some components for products made in England for other markets were also manufactured in China and shipped back to the UK for final processing and assembly.

The China company was followed in 2006 by Fort Vale Pte Ltd in Singapore.

In the UK it was time for another pivotal moment, brought about once more by pure coincidence. It began by my going to the loo at Parkfield Works. Walking back out into reception, I came across Ian Wilson, Dave Smith and Frank Hall on their way downstairs and about to leave the building. "Where are you lot going?" I asked. They were off to Altham, just the other side of Padiham, to look at the Hallmark Cards factory as possible premises for our continued expansion. "Hang on," I said, "I'll come with you," and went to get my jacket.

Ian was finding production at Parkfield Works more and more problematic. Manufacturing was split over two sites – in No. 4 Shed as well as Parkfield. Logistics were becoming impossible to manage efficiently and Ian was determined to move out of Brunswick Street – with its constricted access, awkward for transport – and find modern, new premises. I was not happy with the thought of another disruptive move but I was not as familiar with the day-to-day operations as Ian so did not grasp just how badly the problems were restricting our functioning. Ian insisted that the only way forward was to find modern premises in a location that was well connected to transport routes, that could handle large articulated trucks and had a modern shop floor area where modern machines could be installed with all their associated plumbing – electronic and physical. Of course he was right – we were struggling at Parkfield more than I appreciated.

Returning from our inspection of the Altham Industrial Estate, we were driving past the old Mullard complex of manufacturing works. It was then run by the Dutch company, Philips, and I knew that production was halting and the premises were for sale. It covered a vast area on two adjacent sites. One site was already occupied by Time Computers. The other site, west of Simonstone Lane, was the area for sale. On it was a 5 acre glass manufacturing plant producing 10,000 television tubes a day and other factory buildings. It was a huge industrial area of 22 acres with more estate beyond.

"Stop the car," I said. I left the others and went into the gatehouse, leaving them in the car. The security man obviously did not take me seriously, understandably, when I asked him to ring the top man on site as I wished to discuss buying the factory. He did as I asked and talked to someone at the other end of the phone line for a while, passing

Left: The Mullard manufacturing complex. Outlined in blue is the area I purchased to site the new Fort Vale facility. The buildings around the two tall chimneys are those of the glass manufacturing plant, which were demolished

on my message. I chatted to the security man and, in yet another coincidence, he turned out to be a good friend of one of our long-standing engineers, Malcolm Hudson. Malcolm had been with the company for years and was a well-respected, skilled machine operative.

I waited for quite a time until, after twenty five minutes or so, Ian came into the gatehouse and said, "[Effing] hell Fort, what are you doing?" Hot on his heels, a little man entered from the offices, and passed me a note, saying that I should ring the man in Holland whose details were on the piece of paper. I passed the note to Ian saying, "You've got the ball, Ian – run with it!"

Later, I learnt that others in the property business were also looking at the factory and I realised we had to move quickly if we wanted to stay in the lead for this one. Two serious and wealthy competitors, Howard Rigg and Tim Webber, were already in negotiation and the factory was all but sold. In fact, Dave Smith thought the site had already been bought by them and had not thought to enquire about it because of that.

Dave and I met Howard Rigg on site with a view to splitting the property with him. It was a huge area and way more than what we actually needed so splitting the deal seemed logical initially. Then I came to a decision – we should have the entire site ourselves. Without telling Rigg of my intentions, I came back to the office and told Ian my new plan and asked him to proceed on that basis.

Asking Ian how things were going with the negotiations after several days had passed, I got the answer, "They're progressing very well".

"No," I said, somewhat agitated, "no – we need to get over to Holland immediately and seal a deal quickly or we're going to lose it".

Above: The new office building and reception at Calder Vale Park, Simonstone

We made arrangements swiftly and in a day or so we were both on our way to meet with the Philips team and negotiate the purchase. The price was settled at £4 million sterling. Then the old Fort farming roots played a part.

"Have you heard the Lancashire tradition of knocking a little off the price 'for a Bit of Luck'?" I asked. They were bemused. Of course they hadn't heard of the 'Bit of Luck' tradition. They listened, fascinated, as I explained the custom.

"When a farmer bought an animal from another, he always got a sixpence in the pound knocked off the price as a 'bit of luck' to ease the purchase. It's in case the animal falls ill or under-performs." The negotiators seemed to accept this tradition as a normal part of official negotiations.

"How about a 'Bit of Luck' for the factory – sixpence in the pound, old money, is now 2 ½p, so that equates to 2 ½% - if that's alright with you?"

And they agreed. The net result was a saving of £100,000 on the transaction – for a 'Bit of Luck'. We got the papers through quickly and had bought the factory in four weeks flat. The following Christmas, I had a card from Howard Rigg. It said, simply, "Judas".

Simonstone again illustrates the evolution of the use of facilities from a dying industry, just as did the textile industry. The Philips factory was operated under the Mullard brand and was where television sets were produced.

Mullard Limited had been a British manufacturer of electronic components. The Mullard Radio Valve Co. Ltd. of Southfields, London, was founded in 1920 by Captain Stanley R. Mullard, who had previously designed valves for the Admiralty before becoming managing director of the Z Electric Lamp Co.

In 1923, in order to meet the technical demands of the newly formed BBC, Mullard formed a partnership with the Dutch manufacturer Philips. By 1949 Mullard had produced a number of television sets. The Simonstone facility was closed in 2004 and I bought the site in the same year.

Anne Hartley and her colleague, Liz Shapland, together came up with the name of Calder Vale Park for the site. With the adjacent fields leading down to the River Calder and open countryside beyond, 'Park' seemed very appropriate. Although the 22 acres of industrial site was the main interest, the deal included an extended area of some 59 acres in addition giving a total of 81 acres. The new premises at Simonstone were in a different league to Parkfield Works. The modern construction of the production buildings created vast areas of open space, perfect for neat rows of machine tools with easy routes for handling materials. There was a lot of preparatory work required to get the new premises ready for occupation and, just as with our move to Parkfield Works, we prepared carefully in a planned and controlled manner.

An existing glass furnace facility had to be demolished and existing production bays modified to our requirements. Dave Smith and Frank Hall spearheaded the project. We also needed new offices and an architect came up with a design – which just did not hit the mark at all. Dave found a new architect and I discussed with him how impressed I had been with the glass construction of the Louvre in Paris.

That seemed to get the design going in the right direction. Drawings were produced showing a glass-clad frontage as a spur from a central, round-hub reception with double height atrium and gallery. The curved glass frontage housed a rotating door and the roof was formed by a sloping circle of glass. Detail included automatic double doors to the offices, marble floor and stainless steel and glass balustrades. This would be seen as totally over the top for an engineering works but it was right up my street. An enclosed bridge from the gallery connects to the production area.

There were a few tweaks here and there which I had to insist upon to fine tune the design – some matters of detail which others did not spot but where a small change made all the difference (or not so small in the case of moving the position of the lift). The high quality of finish employed was what I aspire to in my homes and to reflect this in the workplace, although an indulgence, made me happy.

I think that by raising visible quality levels in the workplace, I can influence quality in performance and attitude too. This goes further in practical terms. Automatic lighting and blinds in the offices with air conditioning to make for a comfortable environment shows that we appreciate staff and are concerned with their conditions and wellbeing.

I have always been aware of the importance of good health. I try to spread the word to others where possible and this goes for the workforce at Fort Vale. There is a visiting nurse available on site: we have a scheme to help people to give up smoking; as I write this, plans are in place for a works sports centre and gym and I am reminded of a similar facility established by Amos Nelson for his textile workers in the 1920's. Is that not yet another coincidence? It seems to me that we are forever interlaced with our history somehow – warp and weft.

Work was not completed to a stage where we could start production until 2006 and that was part production only as we stuck to the plan of a controlled transfer. But before the shop floor was fully occupied by machine tools, we had cause for a celebration.

2007 was the 40th anniversary of the founding of Fort Vale. A party was in order. Anne Hartley set to, as always, and began the planning. She provisionally booked a local hotel but very quickly realised that we would be too large a gathering to accommodate. In fact, there was no local hotel that could cope with the numbers that we would have.

Anne had a brainwave – a marquee but not outside. The shop floor was so expansive that we could have a marquee inside, under cover, in the warm. The machines were not all installed yet and there was room. The marquee was lined and decorated: there was an outside caterer barbecuing, inside; a block of plumbed, event washrooms, inside – in fact, it resembled a country fair but inside!

It was an epic party – with great entertainment and the odd compulsory speech, sorry.

The installation of machines, office equipment and personnel continued. Although the intention for a controlled and planned move was a good one, things did not go just as smoothly as hoped. Frank Hall tried to juggle the installation of dozens of machines with production demands. Ian Wilson was wanting machines to be installed and back in production on the same day. The setting up of a modern, complex production machine is very involved. Once in place, the machine has to be levelled precisely. It has to be connected to the power supply, computer network, coolant system, swarf removal system and fume extraction. It became apparent that too much was being demanded of the team: they could not keep up. The move had to be rescheduled if we were to keep machines working efficiently. It was not the same as

Right: The Simonstone headquarters and UK manufacturing centre of Fort Vale prior to the building of the R&D building

moving only fifteen or so much simpler machines into Parkfield Works thirty years before.

The pressure really took it out of poor old Frank. He had delayed his retirement to help with the move to Simonstone. He had planned the electrics, worked through the installations under a huge amount of pressure and was very aware of his responsibilities. When the machines were in, Frank was out. That Christmas he suffered a nervous breakdown, which lasted three months. I don't realise the stress and strain we often put on the team.

Finally, in 2008 the very last person to transfer over from Parkfield Works to her new office at Simonstone was Anne.

Left: Parkfield Works, 1991 – the great team photographed in front of the 'turret'. The bus was fitted out with product displays and toured customers and exhibitions. It replaced a double decker bus which could not drive onto the ferries to get to Europe!

There was a sad end for Parkfield Works because of stupid rules at the time. Empty business property still had to pay business rates. The only solution was to demolish the entire factory. I deliberated over this for months. It seemed to me to be such a waste and totally unnecessary. It could have been used at some time in the future by another company and it is a great regret of mine that an alternative solution could not be found. I finally gave permission for the dear old factory to be destroyed.

Parkfield Works always had such a warm feeling for me but I did manage to keep a part of it in the grounds of my house at Beaulieu. I had built a stone 'turret' in the car park at Parkfield, as a bit of a folly, from masonry of a demolished part of the old mill. I had it transported and rebuilt at home. I also recovered the engine bed stones of the mill's steam engine – huge lumps, the largest of which weighs seven tons. These will form a henge in the grounds at Beaulieu – when I have time to get around to it.

2008 also marked our third Queen's Award – for International Trading. We were exporting 94 per cent of production at this time: sterling work again by the whole team to add to our earlier awards in 1981 and 1986.

The team is all-important, of course. Yes, it is a great advantage to have all the latest technology – and the company continues to invest in this – but having the best people with the knowledge and skill to capitalise on the technology is imperative. People need to have people skills as well in order to function as a team. For example, designers need to be able to talk to production operatives, inspectors or management in a constructive way and with understanding in order to get results. And it works in the many channels of communication between all areas within the company – throughout the entire team.

This illustrates one advantage of the apprenticeship scheme. The training takes place in most departments in the company's operations. An apprentice will experience life in the design office, purchasing, machine operation, programming, etc., as well as having theoretical education. He (or she) will appreciate the challenges associated with each area of operation and be mindful of these when conversing.

And it does work. Where would I myself be were it not for the apprenticeship at Rolls Royce? And where am I now? Compared to what I was like at school – dyslexic and way down on the results sheet, thought destined to be a labourer – my time as an apprentice was a life-changer. I am convinced that the same applies now. Three past apprentices bear this out as they have reached Director level at Fort Vale – David Bailey, Peter Staveley and Andrew Bishop. They were never as bad as I was, I hasten to add: they are highly intelligent and capable. (I have even introduced David to sailing, at Burwain too – which is another result I am pleased about).

I am also very pleased that the memory of my brother, Robert, is perpetuated with the annual apprenticeship award in his honour. He was such a key player in the early days and continued to mastermind production methodology at Parkfield Works until bad health defeated him.

I am proud of the people we have and hope they understand that I am supportive of them. There has been the odd occasion when this has been questioned.

One issue that we had to address was that of representation. Although the directors did take heed of what was passed up to them, the process was not inclusive. This was solved by the setting up of the Employee Forum – a structured group of staff from all departments, including the Board, which holds regular meetings. The establishment of the Employee Forum ensured that any matter needing discussion is raised with and considered by all parties. Pros and cons are elaborated and explained: solutions are often found very quickly due to the wide experience of the group as a whole.

The Unite union became involved with the workforce and tried to persuade them to join. Not necessary – what advantage would it provide: what benefit over and above what the company provides in any case? The debate continued and Ian Wilson sought the advice of an American specialist who had worked with Jack Welch, Chairman of General Electric on similar issues. The American stayed with us as consultant for two days a week for several months in positive discussions with all parties.

At Simonstone, when the votes were counted on whether to accept Unite, the final result was a 2:1 vote in favour of excluding union involvement. The Employee Forum continues to prove positive.

However good the workplace and workforce, a company is always subject to market forces, to supply and demand situations. Sometimes a downturn can be predicted: sometimes not. In 2008 I did see that all was not well with the world. The signs were there that financial disaster lay ahead – not for us in particular but for the world generally and it would be the consequences of the downturn that would hit Fort Vale.

I had already spelled out in a memo to senior staff members at Fort Vale that the writing was on the wall: I wrote to the Chancellor and to several bankers detailing the points that would lead, inevitably, to a financial meltdown. (As I write this, there are equally worrying signs in our current business world.)

History bears me out and the consequence was that one third of our workforce had to be made redundant. This may not equate with earlier statements that I support the workforce and suggests a contradiction. I would point out that unless sufficiently effective actions are taken promptly in such situations, the company itself is threatened and is less

Left: Part of the test facility at Simonstone. I have always maintained that testing products is fundamental to successful performance

capable of a timely recovery and re-employment. Believe me, I hate having to take such action and it always reminds me of the old stagers of the past whom we had to let go. At Parkfield Works, Bill Foulds and Tom Preston had left the company in tears: I will never forget that.

I offered to stop my own salary but the Employee Forum said that I was not allowed to do that: perhaps they suspected I might be thinking of demanding the same of them, which I wasn't, of course. A few months later, with no improvement to the commercial situation, Ian came back to me and said that OK, it was a good idea, so I did halt my salary.

The market began to recover and the company continued with development plans. One particular project was close to my heart. My experience at Lucas Aerospace on the test rigs had shown me just how important testing a product was. Had it not been for my experience with airflow testing at Lucas, one of our star products, the Maxi Highflow relief valve, would never have been the huge success that it was. It was the extensive testing, design improvements and further testing that gave it the advantage over all competitors and made it the industry standard that it became – and still is.

Technical Director, David Bailey, designed and developed a test facility on site, helped to a great extent by John Hird, a hands-on technical wizard. Situated in a separate building for safety reasons, the facility has the ability to test air and liquid flow under extreme conditions that replicate catastrophic disaster conditions in the field. My essential, historical base principal of testing, testing, testing is still respected, practised and continues to be developed further – brilliant.

We are progressive with new technology – a new laser cutting machine, innovative robot-welding installations, the latest in double-chuck, robot-fed machining centres: the advance never slows.

The market improved enough that in 2013 we were exporting 95 per cent of output and were awarded our fourth Queen's Award – for International Trading. Four Queen's Awards – remarkable: what a performance by everyone in the company. I do not know of any other companies in the area with four such awards.

One reason that we were able to increase production was the development of new markets and David's test facility was key here. The US fracking industry was expanding rapidly. The oil produced had to be transported to the refineries but pipelines had not been constructed to do this. The oil was transported by rail in rolling stock that was not really fit for purpose. The emergency relief valves were not going to perform to a high enough rate of discharge or be safe enough to seal the liquid contents in the case of the tank overturning.

Our reputation in the industry resulted in a deputation from Trinity Industries, Dallas visiting the factory in Simonstone. Trinity make the

Below: Ian Wilson and me at Buckingham Palace to receive our fourth Queen's Award in 2013

railcars for Philips Petroleum and many other logistics companies. They were impressed by the production facilities and particularly by the test facility. Development of a valve specifically to cope with the required performance went ahead with orders for astronomical quantities. Testing the new design was crucial in proving performance and gaining the order, as were David's trips to America to ensure a smooth operation.

Market forces came into play once more as the price of oil plummeted. The Middle East were keen to avoid the United States becoming self-sufficient and produced an oil glut, depressing the price and making the US fracking operations less viable. Orders for the rail tank valve levelled off.

Diversification into new market areas was something that I was keen to encourage. "There is nothing more permanent than change", to repeat a favourite phrase. Recognising where our design and manufacturing capabilities might match the demands of a particular market led Ian Wilson to look at the nuclear industry. The high technology of manufacturing processes, skills in design, experience with stainless steel and other high-specification materials, and impeccable quality control at Fort Vale are exactly what the nuclear customers required. A new company was formed, Fort Vale Nuclear Limited, to focus on nuclear industry products specifically, to obtain all the necessary certifications and to qualify for operating in the nuclear supply chain.

Enquiries were received and followed up. When customers visited the factory and saw the modern production machines, the quality control systems and the spotless environment, including a clean room

Left: The Research & Development building on the Simonstone site. The offices have splendid views over the open fields

Right: I chat with one of the machine operators as the Duke of Kent and Ian Wilson talk with Lia Ainsworth, who started as a Fort Vale apprentice and is now qualified. The Duke was on a tour of the factory during his visit to officially open the R&D building

built specifically for nuclear products, it was not long before orders were forthcoming. This company continues to be successful.

We had already had some success with our API coupler. This is a valve used to refuel petroleum road tankers at an oil depot for distribution to petrol filling stations. The design team perfected the design with feedback from the sales team – Kathryn Ball was very effective with customer relations here – and Graham Johnson organised the testing and manufacture. This diversification reduces our reliance on the tank container market, which can undulate wildly in line with levels of global commerce. I am always looking to different markets, just as I did with the gas valve designs so long ago.

Expansion continued and we designed a research and development building, which we built at the far end of the factory site, overlooking the fields that run down to the river. I was involved with the layout with Dave Smith and the building was constructed and finished internally to a high standard – my standard. There was just one amendment that I had to insist upon. At one end of the building was a two storey office section with excellent windows looking out onto – wait for it – onto the back of the factory. The outlook over the fields was faced by the solid, blank wall of the workshop bay.

"It's the wrong way round!" I exclaimed in a heated explosion of incredulity. "Let's get it redrawn with the offices at the other end so that everyone can appreciate the view."

"They will be there to work, not gaze out of the window," explained Dave. Hang on – wrong thing to say, especially to me.

"Research and Development – it's a place of inspiration not desperation – give them the view to inspire creativity. What the hell are you thinking?" The building was turned around. At least the lift was in the right place this time.

I was honoured that the Duke of Kent opened the building officially in 2014. We gave the Duke a tour and I was pleased that he talked to the lads on the shop floor and, particularly, the apprentices. I nearly put my foot in it again.

I have a favourite painting at home of the person I thought was the Duke. I had planned to ask him if he might be kind enough to sign it for me. We were checking with the Duke's office if this would be acceptable. They thought it would be. It was only a day or so before the event that it was candidly pointed out to me that the painting was of his brother, Prince Michael of Kent, and not the Duke. I hadn't known one Kent from another. Imagine the embarrassment if that had not been spotted.

There was quite a party of dignitaries, officials and staff members at the opening. Susan Friedlander was there, too, but little did I know that she would not be with us for much longer.

Chapter 16

A Very Special Lady

I met Susan Friedlander on St. Valentine's Day, 1991 – very romantic. It had been suggested by some mutual friends that we might like to meet.

I was staying at the Savoy Hotel in London, just around the corner from our customer, Sea Containers. It was arranged that we would rendezvous at the hotel one evening. I was looking forward to meeting the lady, having heard favourable comments about her from our mutual friends.

On the evening in question I waited patiently for her arrival. After an hour, I was becoming resigned to the fact that I had been stood up. Surely she would have arrived by now? I could not believe that anyone could be so late for a rendezvous – I would never be. I decided to call it a day and leave.

As I approached the swing doors I paused to let a lady enter from the other side. A picture of style and elegance, incredibly attractive, she stopped me in my tracks and I must have held a stare slightly longer than might be considered polite. She realised, she turned, she gave me a gentle smile and I was mesmerised. An extremely slim figure was clad in an obviously expensive dress that flattered her perfectly. Thick, dark hair, styled impeccably, framed a face with a genuine, attentive expression made friendly with that gentle smile.

Right: Susan Friedlander – my partner and light of my life for a quarter of a century

I nervously enquired and was delighted when she said that she was there to meet me. It was Susan Friedlander. I could hardly believe my good fortune. The issue of being late evaporated. I had been without a partner for ten years. Could this possibly be the end of an era? My fate seemed to be sealed when I saw that her phone number ended in the magic number – 259!

So began our voyage of discovery as we learned about each other – our roots, our ambitions, likes and dislikes. At Rules Restaurant, conversation was easy: she listened and I listened. As we both told our tales, it seemed a natural journey.

Susan was in business – she had an upmarket fashion outlet in Berkhamsted. It was a popular establishment with a loyal client base and was staffed by six loyal and happy ladies, many of whom had been with Susan for years. Her clients were from the upper reaches of society and, as you would expect, there was a good deal of networking involved. In yet another coincidence, it turned out that one of Susan's best clients was Alison in Bermuda – the Alison with whom I had the intimate but brief affair that was the cause of my divorce.

The route Susan had taken to reach her establishment in Berkhamsted had not been straightforward. She was head girl at grammar school. As a child, she had always wanted to become a dancer and danced at every opportunity. It became a serious ambition and she managed to be accepted at the Royal Ballet School, one of the world's great centres of classical ballet training. Sadly, one of her arms became slightly misshapen, slightly bowed, as it grew. This resulted in her being unable to form some of the classic stances in dance and so she had to leave the School.

She was encouraged by her parents to concentrate on academic progress and was expected to apply to university. Although her progress was fine, Susan really wanted to go into the clothing industry. Her parents were not happy about this: the clothing industry, even the fashion industry, was not considered desirable as a career path. They insisted on Susan acquiring some basic secretarial skills and sent her to the Lucy Clayton School, Knightsbridge. Her own true ambitions won out, however, and she put her performing skills to good use by modelling. Once in the industry, she started off as a management trainee in Harrods, becoming a fashion buyer for the store, before establishing her own outlet.

The shop was called 'Susan Douglas', the latter name being that of her son from a marriage to Ari Berger. Following the failure of this relationship, Susan then married Norman Friedlander, in whom she had a loving and supportive partner.

Tragically, Norman died after contracting an infection following a successful operation for a brain tumour, so I was meeting Susan as a widow, on her own and looking for friendship and support at a time of need.

I, too, was looking for friendship, or dare I say love, and support and so we were sympathetic to each other's needs and feelings. As Susan learnt a little more about me – my Northern roots and industrial background – I wondered if she would stay the course or decide I was too 'cloth-capped'. She did not seem the type to be happy with life in rural Chatburn or the mill towns of Lancashire. My northern friends could not see it working at all – a beautiful, stylish lady with airs and graces and Ted the industrialist? Still, I was going to try my best to make it work.

Sailing on the Solent meant that I was spending a lot of time in the South and travelling down from Chatburn almost every weekend. Susan was busy with her shop on Saturdays but I would stay with her in London, at her house. Then, just as had happened to my father's mill in Colne, the lease on Susan's premises ran out and the leaseholder would not renew. So Susan decided to close the business and ceased trading altogether. It was a wrench for her and I realised the business, staff and clients had meant a lot to her, giving her a standing in society. I was disappointed to hear her say that she felt that she now "had no status in life" after losing the shop. I would have to try and counter that feeling and reassure her that closing the business did not lower her esteem.

It made more and more sense to start looking for a house in the South – and around the centre of sailing. Susan was a great partner in the hunt, weighing up the pros and cons of each property we viewed and having an eye for features that I might overlook. It was the time of the Lloyds Insurers crash. The financial climate was changing: the

Right: Dinner on board HMS Warrior in Portsmouth at the Royalist Regatta. Here with the First Sea Lord, Sir George Zambellas

*Left: One of the
pools transformed
with a jungle
feel – elephants
and flamingos
in residence*

writing was on the wall – this was the time to buy. Houses that had
been second homes or holiday homes became available at some very
attractive prices.

We very nearly bought a small property, in Cowes, which we could
have obtained for £120,000 instead of the £150,000 that it had been
a little earlier. I am so glad we did not. Eventually, we started to look
in the vicinity of the Beaulieu River and soon realised that there were
some wonderful properties there. Some were available around the
village but better ones were downstream, nearer to Bucklers Hard and
thus closer to the Solent by boat.

We particularly liked one house on the market with Knight Frank
& Rutley (as was) and the agent showed us around in a manner that
might have been described as less than enthusiastic. I don't know if
it was my northern accent or the fact that I mentioned that I had an
engineering company but I got the distinct impression that he was not
at all convinced that this was a genuine enquiry.

As it happened, a close friend and Burwain sailor, Keith Thompson,
was an International Partner at Knight Frank, Leeds. He happened to
be at their office in Hanover Square, London and overheard the local
agent talking of Ted Fort, a "… penniless engineer…" who had been
viewing this particular property but probably "hasn't got anywhere
near the money" that was needed to conclude the purchase.

"Ted Fort," announced Keith, with a knowing smile, "could buy
that house out of petty cash." He then telephoned me to discuss
the purchase.

Above: Susan and I prepare to leave for a reception from our house in Chatburn

To my great amusement, the agent got back to us rather sharply and was most attentive after that. He had certainly misread me. I love it when people get it wrong and have to back-pedal. As it happened, Keith was actually exaggerating somewhat and I just managed to scrape together the £1.25 million for the house and only after he had managed to get a £50,000 reduction on the price.

This would also be, of course, a huge move and a pivotal moment for Susan. It was a lot to ask of her – moving in with me to create a home. Her classic remark was, "If you really want to buy this house, I'll give it my best shot".

I bought the house and am so glad that I waited until that particular property was available. The location and aspect are perfect and, in my opinion, the best on the river. The long lawn in front of the house slopes down to the salt flats of the riverbanks. As the sun rises, the glittering reflections on the water bring the river to life. At night, the moon can do the same. I still gaze over the water and wonder how on earth I managed to get here and I appreciate just how lucky I am.

The purchase was only the start of what has become a continuing programme of improvements and projects for Susan and me. When we moved in, the first thing that we had to address was the legacy of the previous occupants who were bird breeders and fanatics of non-native species, such as flamingos of all things. Pens of all sizes, shapes and states of disrepair had to be removed. Over the years, the area has been developed by improving the water supply system in the bird pen areas and creating a series of four large pools. They each have their own character with different planting and installations and features – elephant fountains and pink flamingo statuettes in one, in homage to the previous aviaries. I was not sure about the pink flamingos, which

Right: Susan and I, with dogs, Bella and Suki, relax in the garden at Beaulieu

were an inexpensive, impulse purchase at a flower show, but Susan was right again and they fit in well with the scheme.

The house was built in 1928 and I am the tenth owner. It was 1993 when we moved in so, to date, that is 24 years and counting. No others lasted more than 15 years and most a lot less. I put this down to the difficulties and expense of running a 28 acre estate with all the associated hassle and problems.

Susan was excellent at managing it all with me, and helped enormously in bringing my ideas to fruition, and fulfilling those of her own. Often it was difficult to keep projects and contractors or staff on the right path. Where I might lose a little patience, Susan would always have a calm and ordered approach, keeping me calm too as she worked through a solution to whatever the issue might be.

I always had a project on the go in the grounds and after all these years I still do. I commissioned a garage, office and boardroom complex as a major project. The swimming pool, however, was installed by a previous owner and has a humorous story attached. It is huge. It is 20 metres long. The contractor, left to his own devices, misread the dimensions and plotted out the pool in metres rather than in feet, as was intended. The pool, therefore, is over three times longer, wider and deeper than designed! I believe the owner only paid for a pool to the dimensions on the drawings, not as constructed. It takes a lot to keep it heated but I do have some solar heat-collectors on the pump house roof to help.

Susan's eye for style and quality improved the house throughout. Fixtures and fittings are the finest and additions to the structure include a breakfast room and a garden room. Antique furniture from a fellow sailor, Charlie Wallrock, has been added to complement Susan's designs.

Susan also addressed the house at Chatburn on her visits north. She worked with architects and designers to modify the house dramatically. Clever layout changes and sympathetic interior designs transformed the upper floors of the house into a series of grand suites and bedrooms in a way that I could never have imagined.

The grounds of the house in Beaulieu have been cleared and re-planned whilst retaining the woodland areas in appropriate locations. Planting has been extensive and Susan and I developed a wide variety of trees, each marked with a plaque with the species, our initials and date planted. I find it hard to understand why no previous owners planted trees. I am passionate about it. There were no holm oaks, no capaltas, no white beam – I could go on. Trees absorb carbon dioxide and so are good for the atmosphere. It has been a joy to watch our trees grow and mature. Some now are tall and splendid and bring back memories of our time together.

Many species of trees have been planted in our gardens at Chatburn and Beaulieu

Above:
Wellingtonia,
25 feet tall

Below:
Swamp Cyprus, now over 27 feet tall

Above: The top of a church spire from Nelson, Lancashire, rescued after demolition and rebuilt in the garden

And my little structures – how many people have in their garden the top of a church steeple? – or a chapel wall to form a vegetable garden? – or an Aztec-inspired machinery store? These structures are made from the recovered stone from Lancashire – various churches, including one that was near my home in Chatburn, and stone from Parkfield Works in the form of the rebuilt turret that used to stand in the factory car park.

One aspect of my working world which faded away as the scale of Fort Vale operations grew is the design work and draughtsmanship. I was no longer involved with the pen-to-paper stages of product development. This was, of course, because pen and paper no longer were the tools of the trade and I am not computer literate. I did miss it and so I began to develop stylish designs for domestic products. These were items such as book-ends, door stops, pen or pad holders and umbrella stands. They were items made to my high standards, usually in stainless steel, perhaps gold-plated. They might be items I could not find of a sufficiently high quality in retail stores. I would draw up the detailed designs on my drawing board, which I still have and use, doing any calculations required on a slide rule. These were then produced in the factory.

I also collect mementos and installations inspired by my travels. A statue of Buddha; a Vietnamese urn; a statue from Italy; a stainless steel spherical water feature from the Chelsea flower show and a sculpture from Croatia – and the Aztec wall.

And hens: as I had at Lancashire Ghyll, we have them now at home in Beaulieu but the hen huts are of a somewhat better build and the hens are free range. They provide our eggs.

I grow all the vegetables and flowers for the house or, rather, the gardener does. I do get involved and suggest what we should be growing. I am keen to see all the plants in neat rows, in the greenhouse or outside, to true Fort standards. Again my family roots come to the surface as Grandfather grew all our vegetables at the farmhouse. He used to give Robert and me jobs to do – fetching and spreading fertiliser, or "muck" as he called it, or weeding or picking – there was always plenty to do. So I do understand what is involved in growing and am appreciative of the effort.

Below: My design for a stainless steel pen holder

Susan loved the expansive borders of flowers. They remind me of Mother at Lancashire Ghyll in her garden, surrounded by colourful blooms. Mother did a marvellous job of creating impressive displays in a farmhouse garden in difficult conditions, half way up a hill stretching to moorland with its harsh weather. Those early years: the impressions they left, the experiences gained, their legacy, they never disappear.

We have the best in garden maintenance equipment: it is needed to look after the 28 acres and it is housed in stone-built, bespoke sheds, the Aztec village. Hard standing helps to keep all working areas clean and tidy. Paths are edged with kerbstones or with laser-cut, decorative borders. I even have a small road sweeper to help keep pathways clear. Railings are detailed with laser cut infills of my coat of arms, a Lancashire Rose or a Star of David in recognition of Susan's faith.

A long jetty stretches from the garden to a pontoon where I tie up the Aquastar motor yacht and the rib dinghy which can whip me across to Cowes in twenty minutes or so on a reasonable day. The location is important here, too, as the water off the pontoon is a minimum of 7ft 6ins deep at low tide – so quite a large vessel can moor up there.

The whole estate is kept, I insist, to my high standards of finish and maintenance. If I see something that is obviously wrong, tatty or neglected, whatever it might be, I have to say something. I will never understand how people can walk past peeling paintwork or a blocked grate and not do something about it. It beggars belief. I wonder what their own homes must be like. Susan used to calm me down and bring me back to a reasonable level of response. The staff in the house and in the garden really appreciated how she helped in such a situation. I have to be careful to manage my natural way of making people jump to get things done when irritable.

Learning more about Susan, much later in our partnership, I discovered that her health had suffered terribly. In 1976 she had been diagnosed with Hodgkin's disease. A Dr. Philip Goodwin was at a dinner that Susan attended and spotted what he thought was the problem. He was right and the treatment he had her take probably saved her life. She never fully recovered, though, to perfect health. Although she was a very gutsy individual in hiding her problems, she was always a little fragile, health wise. We spent quite some time

Above: Reclaimed stone features that I erect in the grounds are a particular delight

Left: Taking a ride out for lunch in a large helicopter of the type used in the Queen's Flight. I had bid for the adventure at a charity auction. The pilot said he would not land on our lawn again – it was too small

in various hospitals and consulting rooms over the years, becoming all too familiar with the Harley Street area of London. One cannot underestimate the importance of good health and I was adamant that Susan had the attention of the very best practitioners.

So here we were, new folks in a new neighbourhood, in a new social world. We knew some locals but not many. Would we fit in with the Beaulieu set or would we not be socially acceptable? I had no way of knowing. I did know that I had found attitudes and assumptions to be different, certainly, to those I had known in the North. Judgements were made quickly and not always accurately, as I had witnessed with the estate agent. We did make some adjustments. Susan insisted on an engagement ring. Society in Beaulieu was not perceived we thought to be ready to accept a couple "living o'er t'brush" as it was termed in Barnoldswick. I was happy to comply although there was no doubt in my mind that marriage was not on the agenda. The thought of Susan's wayward son inheriting any part of my efforts made it even more certain.

I have made some really close and treasured friends in Beaulieu but other neighbours are rarely seen. Some are '90 day men' and can only be in this country for that period without a serious tax penalty. I am sometimes regarded as a bit of a joke – "Here comes old Clogs again!" – the metal basher from the Midlands (they can't even get the geography right). They tend to brag of their wealth, their Eurocopters, and their Falcon jets.

"Yes," I reply, "you might have the trinkets but you can't afford to live here. I can". They tend not to talk to me again following that response, which amuses, but does not worry me.

I have always paid my taxes and see tax as a way of supporting society. As my friend, Lord Lee, wrote recently, "I don't mind paying taxes. At least I know that I am helping to build two aircraft carriers". I have regular meetings with Lee and his group of keen players in the stock market. We try to ascertain where the world is going and how it might affect our investments. It all helps to generate the wealth that keeps the country ticking over – if you play the game responsibly, that is.

Having a 28 acre estate comes with a proportionate number of problems. It takes a fair amount of time and effort to organise and maintain. My standards are high and I insist the same of staff. There are problems to overcome but I do have that capacity, that ability to solve whatever is thrown at me. I don't think that the previous occupants did have the same capacity for problem solving, or the required wealth, as no period of occupation equals that of Susan and me.

I felt really at home at Beaulieu, in fact we both did. Although I kept the house on at Chatburn for visits north to work at Fort Vale or

Below: Susan was the perfect hostess

sail on Windermere with Graham Murray, Beaulieu was our base, and the house we called 'home'.

From home, we travelled far and wide. We stayed in top hotels in top locations, with friends whenever we could. We did enjoy going away in company. Our adventures included many introductions and meeting new people was always a pleasure. Typically, though, there were occasions when Fort put his foot in it.

I do revel in meeting famous people and I'm afraid it's my nature to try and impress them. My enthusiasm in engaging with them can be my undoing if, for instance, I am 'over the top' with my self-importance. Susan must have been on tenterhooks at times, just waiting for the next faux pas. They were never long in coming.

I have already mentioned meeting Her Majesty when collecting the first Queen's Award and I have met her again several times since then, at Buckingham Palace events, such as a fundraiser for the Outward Bound Trust, whose Patron is the Duke of Edinburgh. As I shook his hand, I burbled on, telling him that I had shaken the hand of his wife many times, now. "Fort, you're swanking," he said, seeing right through me, and walked off.

And sometimes, when I try to impress, I am simply not believed. I was once asked if I had a boat. "Actually, I have nine," I answered, quite truthfully at the time. "What medication are you on?" queried my disbeliever, before he walked off, convinced that I was a sandwich short of a picnic. Swanking doesn't always come off well.

One particular incident was when I met Prince Albert of Monaco. I was attending a function about climate change, a subject on which I am keen to inform others as it is so important. The Prince has a foundation with a similar philosophy. The clanger? Instead of the correct etiquette of addressing the Prince as "Your Serene Highness," I came out with "Your Supreme Highness".

We survived. Susan usually either stopped me getting into too much trouble or managed to get me out of it.

A particularly memorable trip was the World Leaders Symposium in 2010, a ten day event held on the Silver Wind cruise ship in the Black Sea. Most of the attendees were from American universities – Yale, Harvard and the like – or high-level international industrialists. I felt distinctly low-level in comparison. The main speakers included dignitaries such as Condoleezza Rice, former US Secretary of State, William Perry, former US Defence Secretary, and Mikhail Gorbachev, former Soviet President – as well as top government ministers and industrial magnates from the countries visited on the cruise. I cannot understand to this day how we managed to attend this event – it was probably through Susan's contacts in the travel trade.

The symposium began with three nights at the Moscow Ritz-Carlton

Above: A stainless steel ball water feature – not favoured by Susan who asked for it to be moved to a less prominent location

and a tour around parts of Moscow not often open to visitors. There was a gala dinner with Gorbachev. Then a chartered jet to Istanbul where we boarded the luxury cruise ship. The main speakers gave their talks aboard the ship. We visited Batumi, Georgia; Sochi, Russia; Baku, Azerbaijan; and Yalta, Sevastopol, and Odessa in Ukraine before returning to Istanbul. At every port of call we were greeted by a brass band as we walked down a red carpet. The submarine base in Balaklava, by the way, was an unbelievably impressive facility – something out of James Bond.

It was a fascinating experience and I found it hard to believe I was moving in such esteemed circles. Each one of the speakers had such a powerful presence when entering the room: they were focused, knowledgeable, sharp and commanding. It was almost overwhelming and so interesting to talk with such high-level personalities. Although I felt very 'low-level' compared to these individuals, Susan could hold her own in conversation with any of them.

Perry talked of his time in office and his efforts to contain the threat of a catastrophic nuclear conflict. He spoke of the possibility of such a catastrophe occurring by accident. When Under Secretary of Defence under President Carter, he was awoken one night with the news that 200 intercontinental ballistic missiles were heading towards the United States: a heart-stopping situation. What was he to do? Awake the President? Put the US missiles on a retaliatory status? After twenty minutes, which much have seemed like a week, he received a phone call that it was a false alarm. It could have resulted in the end of civilisation.

Some time after returning home, we were pleased to meet Gorbachev again when we were invited to his 80th birthday celebrations at the Albert Hall.

It was on a trip to the South of France that we discovered a perfect bay on a perfect headland near Antibes. It is a wonderful spot, with the best views and we decided that if a property came up for purchase we would have to buy it. The location was Juan Les Pins – about the most upmarket and expensive area of the whole region. Susan's sister Beryl had a house nearby which was an additional plus for her.

I was driving with some estate agents from Savills, along the coast from the Belles Rives one day, on our way to the Eden-Roc. Gazing out over the Mediterranean on a glorious day, I was suddenly inspired. "Stop!" I said. This is where I want to be." I had just had one of those 'this is it' moments. The location was perfect, as was the lie of the land that caught the evening sun. The fantastic view over the sea could not be bettered. Properties there were slightly elevated to make the most of the view. If we could find a house far enough away from the coast road to be out of earshot of traffic noise, that would be perfect.

One more coincidence now – Susan had heard of a house for sale

Below: Together in the garden at Chatburn

from her sister in the very location I had my eye on. Beryl's estate agents had all the details. She had been told that it was actually for sale because the lady who lived there had died and the family wanted to sell up. Susan had visited the house only the day before I passed by the location.

It had been built in 1971 and belonged to a Madame Fink, who had died at the young age of 62 years whilst on holiday in Mauritius. The Finks had a large clothing factory in Frankfurt, Germany, employing some 4,000 people. Coincidentally Susan knew her well. She used to buy from Madame Fink when she was a buyer at Harrods and also for her own shop. The Fink family also owned 50% of Louis Feraud, the famous fashion house.

It was all perfect: Susan loved it and so did I. It was not just the house that was for sale but all of the contents were included as well. The children of the family had several other houses for sale and wished for a clean break: everything had to go. The family name began with the letter 'F' so all the monogrammed linen, towels, cutlery and the rest, were correct for me too.

Some very expensive fittings, furniture and paintings were all part of the arrangement. I did ask Angela, of the estate agents, VIP, if she was sure that they wanted to leave all these valuable contents and she confirmed that they just wanted rid without the burden of a pile of goods. The Fink family were extremely well-to-do, of course. Their house in Gstaad was bought by Bernie Ecclestone.

So now we had a lovely bolt-hole in the South of France, from where I could go sailing in Cannes or St. Tropez. The weather there was perfect for Susan's health.

The reason we visited that part of France all stemmed from sailing, as you may have guessed. Huge parts of my life have been influenced by and had direction determined by sailing. This particular series of events started in Cowes. I was looking for a boat to sail there and of a class that was part of an established fleet with regular racing. The one which was recommended to me was the Daring class. My contact there was Nigel Harley, who used to work on my boats in his yard on the island. He knew of one for sale from a group of four barristers for the sum of £16,000. The barristers, Nigel said, were each planning to give their wives a Christmas present of four thousand pounds. In the end, I changed my mind and put down a deposit for a new boat instead of a second hand one.

I don't know how it happened, but it appears that it was understood by the vendors that I had made an offer to buy the boat through Nigel and they considered that offer to be binding, as Nigel was my agent, in their eyes. They threatened to sue for the full amount. Here I was, northern tin-basher, up against four seasoned barristers. I consulted my Lancashire solicitor, Simon Newton, who I had been using for years. Was there a way out?

"I know," said Simon, when briefed on the situation, "we'll go for a court case in Blackburn." It worked. The highbrow London barristers were not up for a trip north of Watford and the case never materialised.

As it happened, I was saved from buying the new Daring as well. I say 'saved' as I came to realise that the Daring is not a nice boat to sail – well it's not for me, anyway. The boat builder went bust.

So I was tempted by the Dragon class. I had, after all, sailed one at Abersoch many years before and there was a good fleet at Cowes. From the fleet members, my fellow sailors, I had heard about the famous Régates Royales for Dragons at Cannes. It sounded to be a good, competitive fleet and I attended for the first time with Will Willet and Iain Morrison. It was a fantastic event and we enjoyed the sailing and the area so much that we continued to attend the Régates Royales for the next twenty years. Susan loved it too – the area, that is: she never sailed.

Hence the house purchase. So, if it had not been for the fact that the purchase of a Daring fell through, leading to my getting a Dragon, I would not have the base in France which has given so much pleasure to Susan and myself. A huge portion of my life would have been totally different.

Our travels in France and Monaco brought us in contact again with the retail fashion world. Susan became very interested and involved with a designer in Monte Carlo, Veronik Alexandre. It was good to see her interested and enthusiastic. Veronik wanted to open a boutique and Susan was keen to support her, so we loaned her some capital to give her a start.

The boutique, 'Pretty You', was fitted out to an impeccable

standard – the highest. Opening night attracted Monte Carlo residents of appropriate standing. The shop was fronted by a row of brand new, pink motor scooters, in 'Pretty You' livery. The stock Veronik was selling was extremely top-end: I could not believe the price of some of the handbags – many thousands of Euros. But Susan admired Veronik's taste and style. She supported her with plenty of shopping trips. I couldn't help thinking that I was paying for all this. It was for Susan: I justified it to myself with that.

Unfortunately, the bottom line was not good. Even with a second outlet in Monaco, the concern was losing money. After several years I had to recall my loan notes. It was a shame but it could not continue. I felt that I was being taken advantage of.

Above: In Rio Carnival costumes

We travelled to many countries together – something we loved to do. On a tour around South America we were talking with some fellow travellers that we had met in Argentina. They said that we must go to see the carnival in Rio as it was on at the time and should not be missed. A change of plan saw us arriving in Brazil first. We then stayed at the Copacabana Palace in Rio de Janeiro and joined in with the celebrations, fancy dress and all.

It was spectacular: it was infectious. I said to Susan, "Look at all these old men out with young women".

Susan had eyes in a different direction. "Look at all the older women out with young men".

She was actually propositioned at the hotel by a handsome young Brazilian. "I like you very much. If you pay for me," he suggested, "I will come to England and be your lover in London". Although it amused me greatly, Susan did not like that at all and hated me telling the story. But the carnival was great fun and we returned the following year.

On an earlier trip to South America, we flew into the high altitude airport of Quito, which made Susan very ill – she could hardly breathe – and then on to the Galapagos Islands. We were both keen to see the wildlife there and took a trip on a small steamer. Although I had booked a premium cabin on board, the pecking order of the other passengers, who included Lords and Ladies, soon shuffled us down to the lower decks – although I did manage a refund of sorts. The birds and animals on the islands were fascinating and one could get very close to them – they had no fear of humans. We had to stick to the defined paths and there were strict instructions not to try to touch the animals at all. Being able to get so close allowed one to study the iguanas, tortoises, frigate birds and the many other species and I could quite understand how Darwin developed his theories in the 'Origin of Species'. As well as being home to land animals, the convergence of three ocean currents brings an incredible mix of marine life to the seas around these volcanic islands. They were designated as the first World Heritage site in 1978.

We visited many places in South America, including Lake Titicaca, the highest lake in the world and also the largest in South America. Another highlight was a flight over Cape Horn and across the Southern Ocean to the Antarctic.

In Egypt we were caught out by a local scam. On a visit to the pyramids, I accepted the offer of a photograph on a camel for such and such a price. "Get on the camel, sir," instructed the handler and I climbed up into the saddle. The handler got the camel up on its feet and I expected him to take a photograph of me, Lawrence-like, with the pyramids as a backdrop. Instead, he gave the camel's backside a whack and the camel set off at breakneck speed with me hanging on for dear life, bouncing around in the saddle, expecting to be launched into the air at any moment. The camel did not stop and galloped on for quite a distance and around the far side of one of the pyramids where another Arab appeared in our path and got the animal to stop – and very easily too. It took a few moments for me to settle and realise it had been too easy for the man to stop the camel. My suspicions were confirmed when he said, "You must pay extra for the photographs now, sir," and he quoted a price that was twice the original figure from the first man. "You must pay, sir, or you will have to walk all the way back." I suppose I should have been annoyed but it was more amusing than upsetting.

An excursion up the Nile River as far as the Aswan Dam felt very

Right: Susan with her two dear dogs that meant so much to her, Suki and Bella, in the garden at Juan-les-Pins

biblical to me as we travelled through the region of such significance in history. Many of these 'wonders of the world' leave me pondering their origin. How could such ancient civilisations create such spectacular and technically advanced features? When I looked at the precision fit of the huge stones in the walls of Cusco and Machu Picchu or when flying over the Nazca lines in Peru, following designs that cannot readily be seen at ground level, I am fascinated. I can't quite comprehend how these civilisations could have done such perfect work. Was there some outside guidance or, more likely, am I simply not good enough to fathom their techniques? There are lots of theories on all these installations but I doubt that anyone can say definitively just why the lines of Nazca were made in the desert sands, or by whom, or for what use. To my mind these wonders remain a bit of a mystery and perhaps that is how they should stay – as a prompt to the imagination and, perhaps, as inspiration.

I am always impressed by 'the wonders' and like to have a reminder back at home in Beaulieu. I have carved stone effigies mounted in the stonework of two walls – one Inca inspired, the face of a sun god, and the other a Buddha statuette. I call them Aztec 1 and Aztec 2. It's a mixed metaphor of sorts but I like them.

Other reminders in the grounds include life-sized bronze Springboks from Zimbabwe; an Indian rice bowl and a marble planter copied from one seen at the Copacabana Palace Hotel in Rio. There are many others. These international additions to the collection of rescued stone features and contemporary sculptures make for an interesting and varied scene as I wander around the grounds, which I do often.

I also enjoy taking a car on an organised rally abroad. Susan really liked the rallies and navigated from the passenger seat. She saw it as a fun way of getting me away from the rat race and we loved this special time together. We went on several trips organised by the Wessex Cancer Trust and took a Rolls to South Africa twice. When I became less confident at driving on the wrong side of the road, Iain Morrison took over behind the wheel for us. When Susan became too ill to travel – much to her annoyance – Iain and I went on a rally to France without her. It was a huge disappointment for her as it had been planned and booked by Susan over a year in advance. It included accommodation at the Chanel chateau and a private tour of Coco Chanel's apartment above the shop in Paris. She was devastated to miss such an iconic visit in the fashion world she loved so much. The only positive to come from that rally, she said, was that it gave her a break from the hurly burly of life with me around at a time when she was really struggling with health.

Iain Morrison is a fellow sailor, stalwart friend and brilliant organiser: he enjoys driving so is a perfect companion on these trips. Iain has

Below: A Vietnamese planter carved from one solid block of stone, which resides in my garden at Beaulieu

been a wonderful friend for so many years and very supportive in my busy life. He enjoys sailing to such an extent that he will overcome joint problems or other health issues to get aboard and compete with total commitment. He organises so much, so well – a boat may need to be relocated from Cowes to Cannes: crew and accommodation has to be arranged for a World Championship in Australia: new sails are required for the Etchells – whatever the task, Iain has it in hand and often by his own hand. All this often calls for his absence from the long suffering and lovely Raine, his wife of decades whom we try to include whenever we can.

Iain also had a superb relationship with Susan. Her two dogs, Suki and Bella, were very dear to her and, with Iain having two dogs himself, there was common ground. They would talk often. Iain seemed to relate to and sympathise with Susan's every thought or concern. Whereas I might miss a signal of distress or be too distracted by a current event, Iain was always sensitive to an underlying issue that might appear in the hint of an expression. A subtle gesture, a passing comment or simply a combination of circumstances that might rock the boat would cause him to address the situation as far as he could to relieve any stress.

This said, Susan could take a lot, was very capable of standing on her own two feet and giving as good, if not better, than she got. It was just that Iain would listen – be prepared to listen – where I might not be quite so receptive. Susan appreciated that.

Iain was very involved in my commissioning of a Marlow 72 motor yacht from America in 2010. Although I already had the Aquastar 48 on the Beaulieu, I wanted something more comfortable on a longer cruise, to be able to venture further afield. Susan, again, applied her talent to designing the interior. I was delighted with the result and we really enjoyed our maiden cruise in the Gulf of Mexico.

Following a further cruise in the Bahamas, in 2011 I had the Marlow shipped over to the Mediterranean where we have cruised extensively, visiting Italy, Sicily, Malta and Croatia. It gives me great pleasure, as it did Susan, to be able to take friends on our cruises. Where I enjoyed the seaborne aspect of the cruise, Susan was happier in port, visiting the interesting locations or entertaining, rather than the time at sea. Again, Iain's organisational ability would ensure that there was a local guide waiting to show us around the sights as we came ashore or have onward arrangements in place for those returning home. We rarely wanted for anything.

Occasionally, if the numbers made sense, I would charter a small jet for the journey out to meet the boat. Iain would organise the professional crew, any boat transits and winter maintenance to keep

Below: My Marlow 72 motor yacht on a cruise in Croatia

the boat in tip-top condition. As in all the other areas of my life, there is always something that needs to be done.

On our last cruise together in 2014, Susan and I were in Croatia. Again, we had a busy itinerary and lots to do and see. Iain had been busy organising cars, restaurants and local guides to show us around this very interesting country. But, as each day passed, it became more apparent that Susan was struggling. In Dubrovnik, she stepped ashore with her usual grace, but more slowly and with care. On the island of Korcula she was suffering even more. The gutsy lady in her was trying hard to act as though all was well, as she always did. The spirit was willing, as they say, but the body was weak. The body won and, when she had to stop and rest, in need of a wall for support, close to collapse, it became obvious that her health was in a seriously poor state.

Slowly and carefully we managed to return her to the boat. She seemed to recover slightly but it was quite plain to me that she was extremely unwell. At the hotel in Montenegro, Susan was walking really badly and finally she collapsed. Her illness was coming on rapidly. I was so worried that I asked Iain to arrange an earlier departure to fly home.

It was on a Thursday that we landed at Southampton airport. Our Range Rover was waiting in the arrivals area for private charters. Straight from the tarmac Susan went up to London and to the Princess Grace Hospital. It was fortunate that we moved so promptly. The staff at the hospital immediately realised the gravity of the situation and I was relieved that we had Susan in their caring and professional hands. I had to return to Beaulieu as I had Lord Stevens there for the weekend.

The hospital rang me on Monday. Susan had been transferred to the intensive care ward with total organ failure. I was to be in no doubt as to the seriousness of the condition and should be prepared for the worst. They were doing all they could. She was in intensive care for a week.

They were superb. Susan pulled through the low point and began to recover. The episode had taken its toll, however. The usually gutsy Susan seemed shattered by it all, in spirit as well as physically. She was at the lowest ebb I had seen.

In the twenty five years we had been together I had never seen Susan as anything other than in total control, of herself and her environment. She was able, always, to cope and be positive. Now, here she was, in tears, talking about life being too much, too hard to go on with. It was a total shock. It rocked my world. This injury of the spirit was as much a worry to me as the illness itself. Through all her trials and tribulations in life, not just her health problems, she had fought and won. A final straw had broken her spiritual back – or so it seemed. She remained in hospital for a further ten days with constant attention.

Once again, Susan recovered well and returned home. We took

things quietly during that summer. If we had visitors, Susan would quietly excuse herself after a time and go upstairs for a lie down. Again, the spirit was alive and willing but the body needed rest. Over the two years leading up to this point she had been fighting constantly – fighting, fighting. I have never known such determination not to be beaten. But she was on the mend, yet once more. It was remarkable.

By autumn she had become quite herself again. At a doctor's examination she had been told that they thought they knew what the problem was and how to keep on top of it. The doctor was confident and so too, therefore, was Susan. She was on fire. She was doing too much, as it turned out.

November. Following a lovely weekend together, Susan went off to London for a doctor's appointment. The doctor said that she was fine: he would not need to see her for another three weeks and that he was very happy with her state of health. On returning home, she announced that she had been to Harrods and bought three pairs of trousers as one pair she wore had become shiny.

"Why three pairs, though?" I asked.

"If I want them, I buy them," she said, roughly taking a quote from the Duchess of Westminster's daughter, who, when buying a house in Beaulieu, is reported to have said, "If I want it, I buy it".

It was the old Susan. After all the worry, here she was, back on form, running the house, the staff and me too. She was happy, which made me happy and I began to think we were getting back to normal. The following day was another peaceful one at home with Susan enjoying a walk in the grounds with Bella and Suki.

The next day, Wednesday, Susan visited Dr Gareth Morris at the Wistaria Surgery in Lymington, not far away, as she was concerned that she may have picked up a chest infection. She had an x-ray and then popped into town to buy birthday cards. On her return we left for the Nuffield Hospital, Chandlers Ford, where I had to undergo a cataract operation. We were at the hospital from 1pm until 5pm. We returned home to a lovely meal and enjoyed a pleasant evening. She was on good form, planning our 2015 New Years Eve dinner party, a regular event that Susan looked forward to.

We retired a little earlier than usual, due to my needing more rest following my operation. The dogs went running up the stairs in front, waiting on the half-landing to look back and make sure we were following – a nightly ritual. They know where the best warm spot to sleep is – on our bed and we didn't argue.

During the night something woke me up. I struggled, at first, to come round and realise what was happening. Was it a sound? The clock said four-thirty. Was it the dogs? Then I heard groaning. Quietly and carefully, not wishing to wake Susan, I reached across and put on the bedside light. I looked over to Susan who had not stirred.

She lay on her back, stiff on the bed, mouth wide open, her eyes shut. It was immediately obvious that something traumatic had happened to her, something way beyond my knowledge or ability to cope with. She needed help: I needed help.

I quickly gathered my wits and went over to the staff cottage where Martin and Sarah Lockyer lived. It is only a few yards away: I got there in moments. Martin's dog heard me, started barking and woke the household. Martin, the ex-soldier, experienced in handling critical situations, took charge immediately. I was in shock, I imagine, as it all seemed to happen around me – the ambulance: Sarah talking with soothing words I did not hear: Susan on a stretcher: attentive nurses. I had to go in the ambulance – alright, I'm coming.

Susan lay under a blanket in the ambulance. Her eyes were open and she was looking at me over the top of the oxygen mask.

"Are you cold?" was all I could think of to say. She nodded. She could understand me, at least. That was promising. It was 5.15 by this time and the ambulance took us to the A&E department at Southampton General Hospital. The staff were on standby, ready to receive Susan. From A&E she was taken to Intensive Care and we waited for news. Martin and Sarah were with me the whole time. Sarah was a great comfort and stroked my hand reassuringly whilst saying all the right words, trying to put a positive outlook on things. Martin, ever vigilant, was making sure that we heard what news there was as soon as possible, alert to any activity around us. The brief reports we did get were not promising. Then the doctor would hurry away again to continue with Susan.

Susan had suffered a massive stroke caused by a blood clot reaching the brain. Her condition was deteriorating. There was no further treatment that could help, the doctor had said. Susan was leaving me.

The way that this was suddenly and emphatically put to me created an immediate sense of doubt, and guilt. Can't anything be done at all? What about transferring her to the Princess Grace in London? Could the experts there help? I felt that I should be doing something, taking some action, making some decisions. She would never survive the journey, was the response. She would be dead before she reached London – it was an unarguable fact.

By mid-morning, treatment had ceased. Her son, Douglas, had been called earlier, as soon as we realised how serious things had become. He and I went in to see Susan for the last time. There was no sign of life. When Douglas held her hand and I touched her leg, there was no reaction. We stood, silent, with our thoughts as Susan left us.

Chapter 17

A Very Memorable Lady

I had never imagined that it would happen that way – that Susan would go before me. All my future plans and arrangements had assumed that I would be the first to go. This new set of circumstances was totally unexpected and threw me into confusion. I was not prepared for this.

I don't remember much of the journey home from the hospital. I was still in shock, in a daze, but I knew that Susan would never return home with me again.

I was persuaded to return to bed to try to get some sleep. I was being steered through a passage of lost direction.

A similar feeling surrounded me at the funeral. Being Jewish, Susan's body had been taken immediately into the rituals of the faith. Her family arranged the internment at the Western Synagogue Cemetery, North London. They took command, quite correctly of course, but it left me feeling to be an outsider, not of their brotherhood, even though I had been closest to Susan for a quarter of a century.

There were many of Susan's old friends there as well as family. Some were from days before my time; some were common to us both. Friends from the north, from work, from sailing and staff from the house, all came to lend support – and, bless, bless, bless – Joanna brought Guthrie, my grandson. It was wonderful to see them both and I determined to see more of them in future.

The ceremony was strange and alien to me. I was used to the Church of England. The plain casket sat in the middle of the chapel. Words were spoken. Then Douglas, most composed, added his thoughts and memories of his mother. I had written something but was unable to deliver it. I am never good with speeches and under these tortuous circumstances did not even want to attempt to portray my own feelings.

As my proxy was about to read the passage for me, though, I felt I had to say something. I tried to quickly blurt out why I was asking someone else to speak and only just managed to in a clumsy, semi-coherent manner before sinking back into the congregation to hide. My proxy pressed on…

"Today is a very sad day for all of us as we gather to remember Susan. Today marks the end of our gilded journey through life together and many say we were the Golden couple. Susan was my right hand and

was always beside me, supporting me and guiding me.

Through our lives we have helped many people with our two foundations, the Fort Foundation and the Beaulieu Beaufort Foundation, Susan always thought of others before herself, and this will continue.

It is two years since Susan went to A&E in Southampton, in November 2012. Susan always showed great courage, strength and determination – this was her character.

Susan has left a great void in all our lives but the strength of her memory will always be with me, and from that I have the strength to go forward."

I only wish I could have delivered these heartfelt words myself. They were brief but honest. They were right for this ceremony in this place in this company – but, there was so much more to say of this special lady and our life together. I determined to do more in my own way later. "You'll see," I thought.

From the chapel we processed to the graveside. The cemetery was huge and it took some time for us all to reach the family plot, next to her beloved husband, Norman. More words were spoken and the family tossed earth over Susan's casket, as is the way of their faith.

Conversation was sympathetic but awkward and strained at times with those who struggle with such occasions, understandably. There was many a wet eye. Afterwards it was refreshments at sister Beryl's with a good number of the attendees. I remember an array of photographs of Susan, which Beryl had put out and was appreciated by those who reflected on her life.

I returned home with Iain Morrison, who had accompanied me from Beaulieu and would stay for a while. He had been so close to Susan. It was tough for him too.

In London, later, I met Susan's doctor, the one who had thought her health was fine and improving. When I told him the news of Susan's passing, he was visibly shocked and could not believe that she had gone so soon and so suddenly.

My life had changed forever. My rock, my support, my protector in a way, was gone. My guiding light had gone out. I was on my own. There was now no one to prevent my putting my big foot in it, to curb my outbursts or to balance my arguments.

More importantly, there was now no one in whom I could confide and with whom I could discuss the most intimate of concerns: no one so close and so loving to listen, to understand and to help resolve issues for the best.

I had support from friends and from the staff at home. The staff understood. They had been, after all, in contact with Susan the most.

They knew it would not be easy without the guidance she provided. It would need patience and tolerance on both sides to keep things running smoothly.

Friends from all aspects of my life rallied round, as did colleagues from Fort Vale and other companies in the Group. I appreciated and was touched by the sincerity and volume of messages of condolence and kind good wishes.

It was not long, though, before a more unpleasant side of the situation had to be dealt with. "Are you thinking of selling and moving on, now, sir?" an estate agent asked. I was not.

"Would you like to consider a value of the property, sir, in case there's a change of mind? Perhaps £25 million?"

I suppose the man was merely doing his job but I did find it rather insensitive and he got short shrift.

More upsetting were those who played on their friendship with Susan, using it as a lever with which to attempt to prise good fortune from me for selfish gain. I heard the phrase, "Oh, Susan would have wanted it" more than once.

I am still approached with a "Wouldn't it be nice…." request for this or that to be created and dedicated to the memory of Susan – and would I like to finance the project? I am becoming immune to these now.

Then I did it my way. Susan was going to be remembered with a fanfare, a celebration of her life. I wanted to give the opportunity to those unable to attend the funeral, as well of those who were there, to hear more fully about Susan. We would have a memorial service at Beaulieu. A meal afterwards would give everyone the chance to talk of their own memories and it would be an event that Susan would have enjoyed and appreciated.

Below: The Abbey Church in Beaulieu, where I held the memorial service for Susan

The service was to be held at the Abbey Church in Beaulieu and was to be followed by lunch in the Domus in the Abbey grounds. Arrangements were made and invitations sent out for the big day on the 30th January 2015.

The church was a picture. I could not help but see Susan in my mind's eye smiling at the wonderful floral arrangements all around. It was a difficult time again, as was the funeral, but more time had passed and I knew what to expect. That did not stop the wet eye or the lump in the throat, though, as the many attending came up to say hello and tell me how sorry they were. We had been such a close couple, they said. The church was full to bursting with family, friends and colleagues from all points of the compass, 225 in all. Although the occasion was sad it was wonderful to see everybody. Seeing everybody there put a positive slant on things and reflected Susan's ability to touch one and all.

The service was sensitive and appropriate. The choir was memorable. Then we came to the time I knew would be difficult again, the eulogies. There were things I wanted to hear, that I needed to hear, but there were things I did not want to hear. The first two to speak were Susan's sister, Beryl and her son, Douglas.

Beryl said all the right things. She talked of Susan's life before I knew her: of her character, her mischievousness, her talent, her determination, her loves and her final partnership with me in Beaulieu. I smiled, I laughed, I wept a little at times.

Douglas did not mention me. It was as though I did not exist. He talked of Susan's prior loves, not mine. The mother-son relationship came across very genuinely and others would have appreciated his words. I did not.

I was to be third to speak in the order of things but could not and did not wish to try. This had been decided weeks before. My good friend, and good friend of Susan, Christopher Lee, was going to speak on my behalf. It was the correct decision. Had I tried, it would have been a shambles. This was no engineering challenge.

Christopher had taken my thoughts, memories and wishes and written the perfect piece. He could, of course, as he is an academic, professional writer and broadcaster for the BBC. He knew Susan too – he could read her character, her thoughts and wishes. Between us, we made sure that we touched on the key points that Susan would wish to be mentioned in remembering her life. We had included the pertinent memories with genuine feeling, referring to our memory of what Susan would have wished to be said, we hoped.

Christopher's professionalism shone through in his delivery. His intonations, the pauses in the flow of words for emphasis, the rising or lowering of his tone, his scans of the congregation – all these added to give just the perfect sense for the occasion. Susan would have loved it.

He then announced that he was going to read out a letter. Christopher explained that it was a very personal letter and that he had persuaded me to allow it. It was a letter that Susan had written to me when she was about to have a serious operation. She was by no means sure that she would survive the operation. She feared the worst.

But these were words from Susan herself. These were her thoughts, her feelings, her fears, laid bare. Christopher said that he had been touched himself with the open and undeniably genuine emotion of the letter. It would be the perfect occasion for Susan herself to confirm her feelings.

He had to pause. Taking a glass of water he turned away from the eyes of the assembled to hide his obvious emotion. A sip later and recomposed he turned back and began to read the letter to us.

My Darling Teddy

Just in case. Thank you for being a major part of my life. For the past 22 years we have shared our lives, the highs and the lows. The wonderful times and some rather nasty times as well. But we weathered our storms and have so much to look forward to God willing.

If anything untoward happens this afternoon I shall be so very grateful that we met. I am very proud of you. A truly special man. A good man. Kind, honest, caring and loving. An honest and generous human being who has been a great achiever and yet retained his values and generosity to others. Remember, I loved you and respected you beyond measure.

I cannot find the words to express what my heart is feeling. I love you and want you to look after yourself.

My deepest love

Your Susan

PS Sorry my office was not properly sorted.

It was an emotional moment but it left everyone there in absolutely no doubt about the deep feelings that Susan had for me. She had never meant for the letter to be read by anyone other than me but I am so glad to have been able to let Susan confirm her feelings for me to the world in her own words.

She recognised and respected that I had 'retained values' and was 'honest and generous'. These are very important points and sentiments that I retain today. I never forget my roots, my family, the early days of struggle to establish myself, and the moral values in life instilled in those formative years. Susan knew that.

Equally, Susan valued the fact that we could help others and that it was, indeed, our responsibility to "pass down the prize of success", as Uncle Phillip had said. With the Fort Foundation and the Beaulieu Beaufort Foundation, which Susan had helped to set up, we are able to give a helping hand to the deserving.

The reading of that letter said so much in so few lines and to so many. Christopher was right in persuading me to let him read it out.

We left the church for the Domus and champagne – Susan would have liked that too. Not everyone could stay but even so the cellar was packed with 160 chatting people – Madeleine had come over from the house in France that she looks after for us with her husband, Daniel. The optician, Fabrice, had come from France too, from Antibes. Our sailing friends from far and wide joined colleagues from the business world and local friends in Beaulieu. The conversations were incessant and buzzing. All there knew and loved Susan.

Jayne Patz had done all the organising from her base in our home office where she works and, co-ordinating with Jan Hoy of the Beaulieu Estate, had arranged a splendid function and a lovely meal. The dining room was bedecked with marvellous floral arrangements and the tables were immaculate. This really was an occasion that Susan would have appreciated immensely. I had managed, I hope, to put on something more akin to our lifestyle than standing in a windy cemetery in North London.

Things settled and I became more used to life without Susan. There are constant reminders of her around the house and grounds so she is never absent, in a way. Susan's style is ever present inside the house in the decoration and the choice of furniture. There are the many trees we planted in the grounds with our names together at the base. All the garden ornaments and features are reminders of our trips to far off lands – trips made together. Even the large stone features in the grounds, the ones that Susan did not fully appreciate, remind me of her through the memory of her critical remarks – "It's supposed to be a garden, not a park".

Above: We took great pleasure in planting many varieties of tree, marking each one with our initials and the date

The clock in the bell tower rings just once on the hour, whatever the hour. When it rang to sound the exact hour of the day it was too much for Susan and she had it altered. I am reminded 'once' more. It was erected to celebrate our first ten years in the house.

And the dogs are still there. I take much comfort in Suki and Bella. They were Susan's dogs and still are. They still prefer the presence of a lady to a man and will wander over to a female for attention first. I continue to allow them their traditional sleeping location on Susan's side of my bed and they romp up the stairs first when it's time. They check that I'm following – as Susan might. She was such an important part of me for a third of my life.

Life goes on – a very different life but progressing nevertheless.

I travel back to Lancashire fairly regularly for meetings on business and finance. The house in Chatburn still needs to be managed. The teams I have at Fort Vale now and in other areas of the Northern side of life are so effective that I rarely have to worry. I do like to put in fo'rpenneth on some projects and suggest new directions – in all aspects of life. I get these good ideas where others may not.

Thankfully, I still have good health and am able to travel around, to walk well, to sail still. I am enjoying my remaining time on this earth or, as I call it, my Quality Remaining Time – my QRT.

I have made some attempt to fill the void left by Susan – without success. I should realise that there will never be anyone that can hold a torch to Susan in reality. There are times when I need a female partner for social engagements and several kind ladies have been good enough to help. I have never come close to forming an emotional relationship

Above: The bell tower constructed to celebrate the first ten years that Susan and I lived in the house. It reminds me of her every time it strikes the hour – just once

although I have made new friends. I am pleased to have been able to have the pleasure of the company of some of my female friends from the Beaulieu area at social events. They are very supportive.

Chapter 18

Health is Wealth

Anne Hartley introduced me to Aquarobics initially in Greece. The prize for winning in the Sunfast fleet at Cowes in 2008 was a holiday for the whole crew, courtesy of Sunsail. One of the activities in the sailing resort of Vounaki where we stayed was an exercise class to music in the pool – water-based aerobics. Anne had enjoyed it and persuaded me to try it too. It was good – exercising in water is beneficial without putting too much strain on joints. I have continued with the classes at a local spa near Beaulieu twice a week ever since.

There is a regular crowd of ladies at each session and we enjoy lunch together after the exercise. These are the ladies I call the 'Water Babes', in jest.

I have had the pleasure of escorting a member of the Babes to a function on occasions. A few managed to join me on my motor yacht for a cruise in the Adriatic. The ladies are great fun and very genuine. We all get on well.

I have always placed great importance on good health. So many of my friends have suffered in one way or another. Some have died – of

Left: My introduction to Aquarobics in Vounaki, Greece

prostate cancer, for instance, and others I have helped by insisting they have a PSA count to see if they may be at risk. Eighty per cent of the male population will suffer from prostate cancer. It is not fatal for everyone – many live with the condition for decades. It is something that can be treated if caught in time, before it affects other body parts, such as the bones.

A clever wristwatch made by the Philip Stein watch company in Miami has been a particularly beneficial discovery. They have been selling a watch since 2003 that is claimed to harness the natural frequencies of electromagnetic fields around the earth and channel them to the benefit of the human body. These frequencies seem to benefit different ailments, from stiffness or joint problems to sleeping issues and other bodily complaints. Over the years I have helped several friends by donating these watches to those complaining of an ailment they are unable to shift. Over fifty watches have been given out so far. They don't work every time – I estimate that twenty per cent of the people receiving them see no improvement. But I know they do work – how? Because they ring up my secretary, Jane, and say, "Help! My watch has stopped working – I'm suffering again. How do I change the battery?"

One of the first to be given a watch, which was highly successful, was the wife of the (now retired) Doctor to Her Majesty, the Queen, and Harley Street practitioner, Sir Nigel Southers. She wrote a lovely letter to Susan and me saying that it was the first time in six years that she had been free of pain.

I am forever questioning friends and staff, asking if they have had a check-up; do they know what their waist should measure (it's half their height – 6 feet, 72 inches – waist 36 inches); their weight; body mass

Below: Artists impression of the Wilson-Fort Sports Centre to be erected on site at Simonstone and administered by the employees

index: I am sure I annoy some of them and I appreciate it's touching on the personal but it is all just my way of making them more aware of health. I'm caring – and helping to my mind, I hope.

Personally, I give my health a great deal of attention. I have a small blood pressure monitor which I use every week. A masseuse visits twice a week. A check up at least once a year shows any change in the body's condition or performance. Fresh air and a walk are always good – I take the dogs out as often as possible. Dentist and optician visits regularly.

I am hugely indebted to an optician in France. At a regular eye test in Antibes, the optician, Fabrice, spotted an aberration. There was a growth behind my right eye. "It has to be removed straight away – a simple operation at this stage," he told me, "but if we leave it untreated, the growth will spread. You would lose the sight in that eye." The operation was straightforward and, thankfully, my sight is fine, particularly having had the cataracts treated. My sight is, in fact, much improved.

Diet is important as well, I feel. I avoid dairy products pretty much and use soya milk. I have porridge and soya milk for breakfast with fresh fruit and, as a little indulgence, some honey. Another indulgence is a glass of champagne, just the one, on the occasional evening. I cannot have too much wine these days – any more than a couple of glasses and I suffer the next day. The wine has to be of a good quality.

Whenever I am able to influence and promote the pursuit of good health, I will do so. At Fort Vale, we now have visits by medical practitioners and all employees have access to them. Tests are available for many medical conditions, which are best caught early. Encouragement and incentives are in place to help smokers to kick the habit. This approach is one of my duties and just one element of looking after those who work for me.

Ian Wilson is also very keen to promote a healthy lifestyle. The new sports centre, which has been proposed by staff, encouraged and supported by Ian and myself, will be another contribution. Also, it will be administered by the staff members themselves, not by management, so will engender a principle of promoting good health by inclusion and commitment.

There are many small touches that have been introduced at the company and they all help in their way. Taking time off for an appointment can be booked as odd hours now, not as a half or full day. There is a dedicated meeting room for discussion, one-to-one, of personal issues with an appropriate consultant.

Ever since an unfortunate period of time when it was brought to my attention that drugs were in evidence in one of my estate cottages at Beaulieu, new employees at the company, as well as new staff at my private residences, have to undergo a drugs test. This is all for the good of the individual.

Although I have had the good fortune to be healthy and also been able to rectify the occasional problem fairly readily with treatment, I have been touched by the ill health of others around me. Kathleen Bedford, my first love, hid her disease from me and I was not aware that she had suffered until her funeral. That woke me up, somewhat, and made me pay even more attention to health in general.

Brother Robert passed away much too soon. Susan suffered for most of her life but the tenacity that woman had for life was unbelievable. I remember that in Montreux, early in our relationship, she bought me a gift of a tie.

"This is to remember me," she said. "You won't be seeing me for a few months." She was taking herself away for a mastectomy and reconstruction treatment. She had not said a word to me about it up until then. More than once she thought she might not survive a particular operation. Her letter to me, the one that said goodbye "just in case," just in case she did not make it through the operation, the one that was read out during her memorial service at Beaulieu, illustrates that point. She did make it that time, however.

Health is indeed wealth.

Chapter 19

The Duty of Wealth

I have said that I was forty years old when I realised that my responsibility was to create wealth. You need a wealth-creating section of society to help pay for the infrastructure for it to function and the resources for it to progress.

Again, I go back to the times when the textile giants of East Lancashire and elsewhere were creating their industrial might. They were also building houses for the workers, setting up Town Councils, paying for hospitals and water supplies. Through employment, they raised the standards of living above what they had been, even if we now look back on those times as hard. No doubt they were hard but not as hard as they had been previously.

They improved things. I too wish to improve things and I feel that I should do so as a duty that comes with wealth. As Uncle Phillip said, one should "…pass down the crystal prize that comes with success". I apply that not only to the workforce in the companies that I run but also to a wider horizon. I am particularly keen to help the young people of the country get a decent start in life, and give them the opportunity to progress. So often, a helping hand with an ambition or giving someone the chance of experiencing an uplifting activity can make all the difference. I can give them a pivotal moment in their life, which can lead to great things – that's the hope.

I relate this to my own life in the early days. I had huge support from my family. Mother never gave in when it came to my education and pushed me to the apprenticeship at Rolls Royce. She did not give up on her dyslexic son. Father did not hesitate for a moment in buying the Norfolk Street premises as I started Fort Vale. These fundamental 'helping hands' were absolutely pivotal in enabling me to achieve what I have.

Sailing. It was something that David Fleetwood and I simply felt we had to try but that again had phenomenal consequences. I gave myself the chance to sail and not only did it lead to years of enjoyment from the racing and sailing itself but through sailing I met so many great friends (and my wife) and made no end of business contacts. I found that some skills gained from sailing a boat could be helpful in other aspects of life. I believe I was better at some of the skills on the water because of my dyslexia. I could think more laterally, discover alternative tactics that others could not. Planning, tactics, reacting quickly to a change of situation, encouraging crew members, planning logistics for foreign regattas, selecting the best equipment – there are many functions required in sailing, on and off the water, that are relevant in business and private life.

In recognising what these opportunities did for me, a Colne lad with clogs on, I take great pleasure in doing what I can to give other cloggies the best chance in life. It is up to them in the end, of course. Not everyone can get to the top of the tree but I can, at least, give some of them a hand.

I think there must be some 'giving' characteristic in the Fort family genes that I have inherited. Robert was very generous and gave ten per cent of his income to charity. I do not work on a rigid percentage basis alone but I do allocate substantial amounts each year.

So I have set up two Foundations – charities, which are geared to give opportunity. The Fort Foundation was the first and it was established in 1993. It is based in the north of England and aims to help young people there, establishments which support youth activities and local community resources, such as churches and village halls. Church and village communities are always very supportive and involving. They should be encouraged.

As I found sailing to be so influential in my progress through life, I support Burwain Sailing Club, the first club I joined. Not only was the club such an important part of my life but nowadays it has a thriving youth training scheme in place, run by enthusiastic and dedicated members. It ticks two boxes straight away. Similarly, Royal Windermere receive support from me for their sailing academy, which I helped to set up with Chas Ingham, to encourage young sailors. The Royal Thames Yacht Club has a sailing academy and has supporting donations from me, as does the Etchells fleet at Cowes. I have been a member of the Etchells fleet there for over thirty years now. They have an enviable reputation for enabling youth teams to compete at the highest level and this has to be applauded.

Larger organisations that attract my support are the Royal Yachting Association and their own Foundation giving sailing opportunities to the young, as well as the Sea Cadets. Fourteen thousand young people are involved in the Sea Cadets in four hundred centres across the country. They get maritime training by experienced volunteers. Each year, the Royalist Regatta is held to raise money for the Cadets. About twelve teams of eight or so crewmen take on the challenge and Fort Vale has taken a boat for many years. As well as inviting some sailing friends for the two day event, I have always taken Fort Vale staff and apprentices to join the crew. They may not have been sailing at all before but this experience may be just the thing to give them the

Below: I set up the Fort Foundation in 1993 to help young people in the North

THE
FORT
FOUNDATION

Left: The lighthouse at Lepe, at the mouth of the Beaulieu River, that I was pleased to help to plan, design and construct

bug. At least two colleagues have taken up the sport following their involvement in the regatta.

The event also gives the opportunity for the apprentices to attend a formal dinner, the ladies in gowns and the officers in dress uniforms, in a dramatic venue, such as the gun deck of HMS *Warrior* in Portsmouth. When else might they experience such splendour? It is all part of a broader horizon of life, which will stand them in good stead.

The church in Colne, Holy Trinity, to which Huggins and I were marched as children, is also dear to me. Another church, St. Mary's in Kelbrook, is where my parents and brother lie. It is the Fort family church where five generations of the family are buried. Robert spent a lot of time there, tending the grounds and doing odd jobs. I continue his commitment with donations and support.

The second Foundation is the Beaulieu Beaufort Foundation: the name indicates the focus. Susan was keen to extend my support to the area around where we lived. This made perfect sense and we set up the Foundation in 2006. There are many excellent establishments, and individuals too, in our region to support. Sailing clubs are at the fore particularly, again, where encouragement is given to young people. The infrastructure of the clubs generally is important. Projects need a firm base.

Support can go to many and varied causes. A community project to build a new lighthouse at the entrance to the Beaulieu River had a substantial contribution. A new pontoon was required at Cowes for the Royal London Sailing Club and I was pleased to help there. An international boat building training college at Bucklers Hard gives

Below: Susan and I set up this charitable Foundation in 2006

**Beaulieu
Beaufort
Foundation**

young people the traditional skills of woodworking for vessels in a location that once saw ships built for the Admiral Lord Nelson. I could go on.

The point is – to give a helping hand. I rarely sponsor a project, person or organisation in full: I lend a hand. I might put up half, say, of a young sailor's expenses to go to an international championship, if they show promise and if they raise funds themselves as well. I need proof of commitment. Delivering everything on a plate is not the way to build character and determination. Again, I think back to the effort I had to put in to achieve. I was helped, it is true, but still had to work my socks off.

Strangely, with all the wealth in and around the Beaulieu area, all the big houses and big wigs, I am unaware of any other individual who has a foundation. Is it just me and my link to Lancashire's historic values and the influence of the philanthropic textile magnates? Or do my neighbours regard profit to be more important than wealth with responsibilities? They have a different sense of duty to mine.

The funding for the foundations comes from different sources but one is from kind suppliers who might make a donation of one or two percent of an invoice to one of the foundations. I am happy to encourage this with a percentage of Fort Vale profits going to the foundations.

The company has reached a level where this is possible. If we hit a global downturn in trading, which can and does happen, the company has to adjust accordingly. Profits will fall and, proportionally, input to the foundations falls.

Below: Warren Buffet – who has only grown his 1$ share value in 1965 to 6,000$ as opposed to my building a £1 share in 1967 to a value of £35,000 – not that shares in Fort Vale are ever going to be for sale!

Over the years, though, the company has managed to grow and I like to compare our growth to that of the famous player of the stock markets, Warren Buffet. He has Berkshire Hathaway, the holding company. It was started in 1965, just two years before me. If you had bought a one-dollar share in his company in 1965 it was worth six thousand dollars in 2015. Pretty impressive, you might think.

If it had been possible to buy a one-pound share in Fort Vale Engineering in 1967, that one-pound share would now be worth thirty five thousand pounds, a much higher rate of growth than Buffet's and in spite of the fact that we have paid out dividends whereas he did not.

We have no shareholders of course – that is a golden rule of mine and I explained why earlier, after listening to Father and Grandfather swearing and cursing at shareholders' comments following the AGMs at Sough Bridge Mill.

So I have reached a level of significant wealth. In 2015, if I had been a senior executive of a public company, I would have been the fourth highest paid in the country. I was in the Sunday Times Rich List. This was a surprise at the time. I had not realised the level to which I had risen. I thought I would like to have a chat with the compiler of the list, Philip Beresford. I did not want him to think of me as a profiteer: I wanted to give him the fuller story of how I got there and the consequences. I had a meeting with him and his Editor, Ian Coxon, in the Sunday Times offices in London. We had an excellent discussion in which I explained how I had got to the position I had but, more importantly, my plans for the future and how I would like to use the wealth to encourage young people in engineering. The emphasis was on apprenticeship, how one had changed my life and my enthusiasm for maintaining an apprentice-training scheme at Fort Vale Engineering. I hoped that other companies would do likewise and that they too would support a scheme where some eight percent of the workforce was training in apprenticeships, as at Fort Vale. It would make all the difference.

I talked of our recent success in America and the fact that when a US rail tank builder wanted a high-specification safety relief valve they came to us. Our reputation for quality gave us a standing that beats the world. A delegation from Dallas, the oil centre of the United States, came over to visit little ol' Fort Vale in Simonstone, near Burnley, Lancashire. A visit to Fort Vale always impresses. The state of the art shop floor, the quality of design and of production will always win approval and admiration. As Ian Wilson says, "Our shop floor is our showroom". It says it all.

With sterling work and collaboration from David Bailey's design team and comprehensive performance testing giving impressive results, the Americans got the valve they needed and placed a substantial order.

Beresford took all this on board and was very complementary. He said at one point that if there were two thousand Mr. Forts in the UK, it would make the country bigger than Germany.

"You are an industrial hero!" he announced. Hang on. I know journalists like sensationalism and bulling-up a story but this was a bit too much even for me, however flattering. One of the problems in compiling the list, he went on to explain, is the number of individuals trying to convince him why they should be on the Rich List. Here was Mr. Fort taking the time to explain how and why he was there – making it meaningful.

I touched on the early days, some Lancashire background, as I have written earlier, which I won't repeat. Some of Grandfather's business 'Rules of Thumb' came to mind, which I use as a check still.

"Three times wages plus materials equals output and profit," was one.

"Five times materials equals selling price," is another. They always seemed to hold true in engineering, with exceptions of course. The economics of life do not change.

2004	2005	2006	2007	2008	2009	2010	2011	2012	2013	2014	2015

```
.......... 3 x wages + materials
—————— output plus profit
```

Above: Grandad's Rule of 'Three times wages plus materials equals output plus profit' still applies to the company today, very nearly. 'The economics of life do not change'

I quoted some of the early Fort Vale production figures – when I had thirteen men producing the equivalent of 13 Mini saloons a month (about £8,000). A Mini these days is about £16,000 and the output per head is still roughly the same – one Mini per man per month.

Messrs. Beresford and Coxon listened. They took my views and illustrations on board, making notes as I spoke. They nodded: they seemed genuinely receptive. I was pleased to make my points.

One more point I made was how I can perceive an economic change on the horizon. The banking crisis of 2008 was a good example. I have a copy of a memo written twelve months before the crash. I refer to it often – here it is…

> *Dear Martin (Drury) and John (Watson),*
>
> *I would just like to make you both aware of my views on the current worldwide banking crisis. This is affecting banks in Australia, Norway, USA, Britain and many other countries. In my view this is the World's worst banking crisis since 1929. The banks are in deep, deep, deep, trouble, like any business they are very good at reporting good news but my experience tells me they are very bad at conveying bad news. If it wasn't for the sovereign and oil rich states where would the money have come from to bail out the banks so far?*
>
> *I think my policy to reduce my portfolio by 50% has been the correct thing to do so far and if the index goes down to 5750 we should sell all the shares.*
>
> *Kind regards*
>
> *TED*

After all this, Beresford and Coxon, the men who meet such a diverse set of characters in compiling the Rich List, had a clearer, truer picture of me as a person: as someone from a modest background who had to work hard to get on; who cares about the future in wider terms, the encouragement of youth, the responsibilities that come with wealth and social duty. I made it quite clear that I am not one of the overseas, tax-avoiding school. I hope I avoided being tarred with that Rich List brush.

Chapter 20

Concerns for the Future

I have talked of the future and helping young people with their lives: of leaving a legacy for times to come with the Companies and the Foundations established and successful.

The Companies have helped me to reach this position in life through teamwork, dedication, skill in management, creativity and hard work. I recognise and salute that. It makes me very proud to think that men and women – and yes, families – around the world are benefiting from the organisations I have nurtured. I hope that I have looked after them as best as I could. That is my intention.

All my actions and decisions have been based on what I believed to be best for the company, whichever company. Even when it may have seemed that I was being irrational, it was for the best as I saw it. When I gathered together the workforce, who were threatening strike action, on the shop floor at Riggs Tools in Colne and said, "If you walk out of that door, you don't come back in": it was for the best for the company. (That was donkeys' years ago and would not be acceptable today, of course.)

When times are hard, we have to readjust. We may have to downsize a little and let people go. It has to be done quickly. It is always hard – don't think I don't feel it when redundancies are necessary. I still remember the tears of Bill Foulds. The action taken is always what is best for the company. I realise it can seem harsh.

It is my wish that the Companies will continue to be successful in engineering, will remain in Britain under the direction of dedicated management with my basic principles of honesty, integrity and philanthropy remaining as the bedrock. I will do all that I possibly can, in my Quality Remaining Time, to ensure that this happens.

The Foundations also will continue with my basic principles at heart and with the Trustees in place who understand me and can administer the Charity, as they know I would wish it. I am confident that arrangements are in place in both these areas.

There is another area, though, which disturbs me greatly. The planet as we know it is in grave danger, yet there are many I talk with who seem to be burying their heads in the sand. In spite of all the scientific evidence and opinions of intelligent and knowledgeable experts, some people still cannot (or refuse to) see the blindingly obvious.

We are seriously damaging our planet. We are creating huge

problems for future generations. Since the beginning of the industrial revolution, we have been adding carbon dioxide to the atmosphere at an alarming and accelerating rate. The resulting global warming and rising sea acidity will have catastrophic effects on mankind and on nature. A lot of people are unaware of the facts or even choose to ignore them. We stagger along, blindly, to our inevitable, disastrous fate. Unbelievable.

I want to do something about this and the main way how I can help in getting something done is to make people aware – aware of what is happening, what is affecting the planet's health and what they, and society as a whole, can do about it: should do about it. I can't wave a magic wand or install tidal turbines but I can try to initiate a tidal wave of opinion, which will put pressure to bear on those who can make a difference – governments.

The fact that I have a certain status on the ladder of society does mean that I can sometimes reach people of influence. Hopefully, I have an effect to one degree or another and if I can get enough of this vital information across it could lead to them taking action – or getting the ball rolling, at least. I will have done my bit in nudging them along.

Whoever I meet in life, whether Gorbachev, Condoleezza Rice, Prince Albert of Monaco, the Duke of Edinburgh, I like to try to get my point across. Sometimes it works and sometimes I can be told to shut up if I labour a point. Prince Philip was one with a limited time of attention before cutting me off.

Another way I spread the word is through a small booklet of facts and information collected together by Christopher Lee and John Hartley. This is given out at every opportunity and is something I can leave to be read later – sometimes preferable and more effective than listening to me talking.

The booklet is based on a presentation I gave in a debate held at the Master Builders Hotel, Bucklers Hard, in 2008. It contains many interesting and, to my mind, indisputable facts and proof that man is changing the climate through ignorance and irresponsibility.

It is a fact that the levels of carbon dioxide in the atmosphere have increased and are still increasing at an accelerating rate. This has been the case since the time of the industrial revolution when the rate at which we burn fossil fuels started to increase.

In the glacial periods, the level of CO_2 was around 200 parts per million (ppm) and in the warmer interglacial periods the level was around 280 ppm. These levels were maintained on the whole by an equilibrium in the creation and absorption of the gas on the planet. Natural generators of CO_2 are volcanic eruptions, animals breathing, permafrost melting and releasing gas (including methane – another greenhouse gas). Natural absorbers include forests and other plant life,

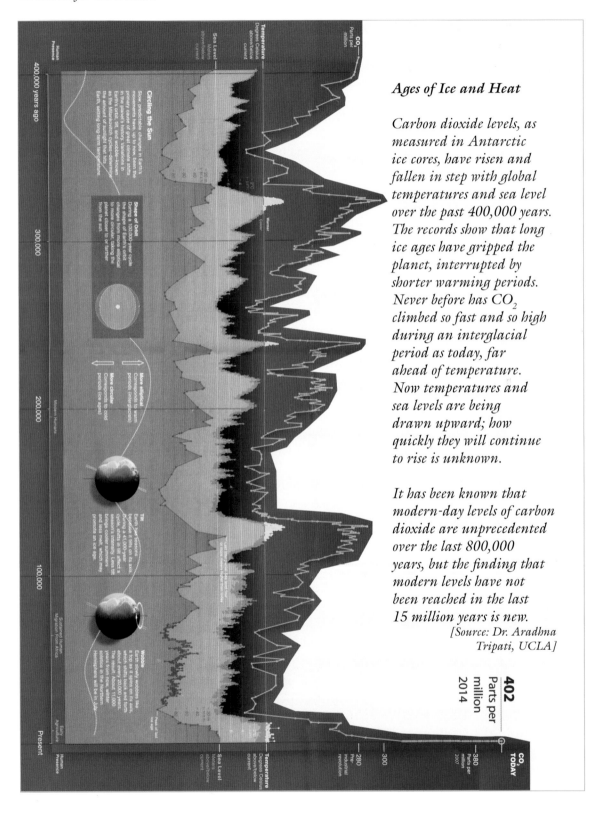

Ages of Ice and Heat

Carbon dioxide levels, as measured in Antarctic ice cores, have risen and fallen in step with global temperatures and sea level over the past 400,000 years. The records show that long ice ages have gripped the planet, interrupted by shorter warming periods. Never before has CO₂ climbed so fast and so high during an interglacial period as today, far ahead of temperature. Now temperatures and sea levels are being drawn upward; how quickly they will continue to rise is unknown.

It has been known that modern-day levels of carbon dioxide are unprecedented over the last 800,000 years, but the finding that modern levels have not been reached in the last 15 million years is new.
[Source: Dr. Aradhna Tripati, UCLA]

*Left: The booklet I
have produced to help
to spread the word
about Man's abuse
of the planet. The
booklets are available
by contacting Anne
Hartley at Fort Vale*

which give off oxygen in return, and the oceans. Man has upset this balance and at an accelerated rate as population and industrial demands increased: they were met largely by the burning of fossil fuels. Levels of CO_2 have now topped the symbolic 400 ppm level. Recent research has shown that this is higher than at any time in the past 15 million years, not just more than the past 800,000 years as previously thought. The rate of increase continues to rise. In 2015 the increase was 3.05 ppm per year. In the year to end February 2016, the annual increase had risen to 3.76 ppm. The increase could be partly due to it being an El Niño year, when meteorological conditions can be extreme and cause effects such as forest fires, which destroy areas of carbon sink (World Meteorological Organisation) but the trend is there still.

Burning a carbon fuel produces around three times the mass of CO_2 than the initial mass of carbon in the fuel as it combines one atom of carbon with two of oxygen. Combining with other greenhouse gases, the effect is to raise the global temperature. This, in turn, raises sea levels (2 cms. per year); increases sea acidity, threatening some species by dissolving shell material, calcium carbonate; melts permafrost, releasing trapped methane; causes extreme weather events such as droughts and storms (as higher temperatures mean more energy in the atmosphere).

The current target of a rise in temperature of no more than 2°C by 2100 (UN Paris Climate Conference 2015) is widely challenged as a 'safe' level. Many think that there would be serious consequences of such a rise.

I could go on – I could write a book on this subject but plenty of scientists, men much wiser than I, have done so already. I will simply continue to try to broadcast the figures in the hope that we can generate a sufficiently high swell of opinion to throttle back our destructive effects and find realistic solutions to preserving the planet.

I must try to do my bit to make everyone's Remaining Time – including future generations – Quality Remaining Time.

Index